AM
PARANORMAL
ENCOUNTERS
VOLUME 2 2016

A Collection of Real Experiences
By Notable Paranormal Personalities

STELLIUM BOOKS
Grant Park Illinois

i

COVER ART BY ANNETTE MUNNICH

Special Thanks
to our authors for this volume
for being willing to share their stories
freely and voluntarily.

COPYRIGHT 2016
Stellium Books
www.stelliumbooks.com
All Rights Reserved
Manufactured in the USA

AMAZING PARANORMAL ENCOUNTERS VOLUME 1

Best Seller on Amazon in Supernatural and Unexplained Mysteries since October 2015

Stellium Books are also available on Kindle and often for .99 cents. We hope you remember us for more good reads.

Supernatural

Frost & Flame Trilogy by Rick Kueber

Forever Ash: The Witch Child of Helmach Creek

Shadows of Eternity: The Children of the Owls

Neverending Maddness: A Girl Lost to the World

By Psychic Medium Rick Hayes

Stepping Stones

You're Not Crazy: You Have a Ghost

Reasons for Hauntings
(Spring 2016)

By Annette Munnich

Ghost Journal & Record Book

9 Angels for Prosperity & Abundance

From Deliverance Minister Bill Bean

Dark Force

Delivered

10 Steps to Victory
Spring 2016

From Alan Wright

Through the Veil and Back: Chronicles of a Healer &
Passive Medium

At the Edge of Eternity
(Spring 2016)

Science Fiction

The Convergence Saga by Rick Kueber

The Pale Titan Book One (serial)

The Genesis Project (serial)

Fiction

By Shannon Anton

My Name is Rose: Diary of a Serial Killer

TABLE OF CONTENTS

A Structure Of Fear

By Rick Hayes

I begin this chapter with a question. How long would you stay if paranormal activity was a constant in your home?

As a psychic medium, activity for me is simply a validation of acknowledgment that has been a part of my entire life. I live a normal life just as you; with the exception of understanding the abilities given to me are also a benefit to better understand why activity of the unseen occurs.

For the past 15 years sharing my abilities with the public, life has also included many requests to assist in paranormal investigations and individual requests. Among the many, this particular case was an opportunity to remove the negative and change a family's quality of life.

My office received a call from a family who requested help as soon as possible. Within a few minutes of speaking with them, my assistant walked into my office and shared "You need to help this poor family as soon as you can. We scheduled a date and time within the next several days and committed to visiting their residence.

1

As we traveled to the location, I could not help but notice the serenity and warm sun on this day. It had been an unseasonably cool spring for the past several days, but this day created joyful warmth. Upon arriving at the residence, we both acknowledged how quaint and neat the appearance of the home was. I also noticed sitting on an adjoining property what appeared to be another building. For reasons only my abilities can define, I felt an unpleasant sense while looking at the adjoining property. My best description was I felt negative energy.

We walked up the small path to the door and were graciously greeted by the husband and wife. With an invitation to enter their residence, we proceeded to the living room where another person was sitting on the sofa. With a smile, the older female shared a "Hello, so nice to meet you. I am so glad you are here!" I noticed that she had her toe wrapped in a bandage and moments later found out why.

The husband, wife, and what I later find out is the mother sitting on the couch, begin speaking excitedly with expressions that combined fear with negative conversation. After several moments, the husband began to explain.

They owned the property next door (the building I had felt negative energy upon arriving) purchased when they bought their residence. Their hopes and dreams were to convert the building into an apartment for residual income with the mother being the first tenant (the lady sitting on the sofa with a wrapped toe). After a few months of renovation and decoration, she moved in with anticipation. Within days – she moved out in fear.

Without a pause in the conversation, mom begins sharing her experience and why she was so afraid. It began with her hearing noises, followed by what appeared to be growling. Soon items begin to move, and all the blinds in the residence windows (approximately 7 to 8) would roll up at the same time. The final experience had her running to her son's house in fear during the night. While standing several feet away, a decorative plate securely on a wall suddenly slammed down on her toe. With tears in her eyes as she shared her experience, she whispered: "it is evil". I knew I had to do something for this kind family.

As we approached the front door to what was now an empty apartment complex, I felt the energy within. As I opened the door and begin to enter, several flies landed on me. The inside was as neat as a pin, so the presence of flies was a mystery. We continued in and noticed the apartment was an open concept. The bed was in the far corner, the open kitchen divided only by a counter island, with the living room in front. My assistant stood with me in the middle of the room holding a video camera to record. The owners stood by the entry doors like soldiers at Buckingham Palace. Within minutes, I was connecting with a presence.

He was an older male spirit appearing to me as a full body apparition. After an acknowledgment, he relayed the message "I am glad you're here. I can help you". He shared that he had lived "over the hill in back and through the woods" many years ago. He also stated that this place we were in had the vision of being spiritual, but it soon changed. Suddenly, I heard a growling laugh coming from a closet. It was time for me to meet whatever this was and take control.

I acknowledged the presence and as I so often do in this type of situation verbally stated: "Thank you for acknowledging your presence, now I will respect you if you respect me". My response shared that I was going to take control. Moments later, several loud knocks sounded from the closet. The older male spirit stood in the corner saying "This is our problem". I suggested the husband and wife step outside and not to worry, I was about to nip this in the bud.

My assistant chose to remain with me, which I admired. With the video rolling, I begin to speak with the spirit. Often I will share that positive overcomes negative every time, to know that you are in control, and to believe with total confidence. I also share that negative energy feeds on fear and doubt, and this presence was about to find out there was not going to be any fear around here anymore.

At one point the spirit attempted to shut me up by what felt as if someone was straining my throat. I struggled to speak, and my assistant asked if I was ok. I nodded my head and as loud as my voice could be at that time shouted "You stop that! It ain't happening!" We later noticed on the video (as my assistant also stated during that time of the recording), that my voice actually changed. Understand, though – NO PRESENCE IS ALLOWED IN MY BODY!

Approximately 45 minutes later, I asked my assistant to step outside as I wanted to be alone in the apartment. What I do alone during these times with this type of presence is confidential. I am by no means a demonologist or any title we like to place on individuals, but I do what many define as pray and share a few things with the negative spirit.

As I walked out of the apartment building, I felt complete calm and a serene energy. I could also see the expression on the owners faces as they both smiled as if they had not been able to for months. As we stood outside, I looked up on the hill behind the building. Along the row of trees and standing by a stump were three children in spirit. One appeared to be an older sister standing close to, I assume, her younger brother and sister. They appeared in period clothing to let me know they lived on earth at a different time. They smiled as if to share that it was ok to play joyfully in the area now.

The husband began sharing with me about the location (I never asked for preliminary details of a location as I believe those in spirit can tell me more than you can). He stated that according to their research the location was once a church many years ago. It began as a community gathering for spiritual uplifting but soon became the opposite. According to research, certain leaders and congregation began practicing negative actions. There is even documentation of the pastor hanging himself in the woods directly behind the building. As the husband shared these statements, I completely understood my experience within the building. I assured them that all was ok now. I instructed them to begin being more positive within their home, to create a bond of love for one another, and to simply believe with positive energy.

Two weeks later our office received a phone call from the 'mom on the sofa'. She wanted us to know that everything had completely changed. The feeling of negativity was completely gone. She and her family were happier than they have ever been. There was peace like never before, and even the building next door felt so much better.

She also told me "I have seen the children playing in our yard. They appear to be happy too!"

I began this chapter with a question for you. I end this chapter with this for you. "BElieve, as you are to be. Be positive. Be grateful. Be generous. Be confident. Be you.

Rick Hayes is a world renowned psychic medium. He is the author of "Stepping Stones," "You're Not Crazy You Have A Ghost," and coming in spring 2016 "Reasons For Hauntings"

Rick Hayes website Lifesgift.com

Reflecting on the Past

By Christopher Di Cesare

"Sometimes you wake up. Sometimes the fall kills you. And sometimes, when you fall, you fly."
— Neil Gaiman, The Sandman, Vol. 6: Fables and Reflections

The fall of 1984 was a very unique and interesting time in the United States. We were nearing the end of the Cold War; the economy was booming; the city of Los Angeles had just hosted the Summer Olympic Games, and the level of Patriotism was unlike anything I've experienced since. It was akin to an entire year of post-9/11 unity, but without enduring the pain, the loss, and destruction that accompanied it. It also marked the first time that I was eligible to vote in an election, and I – as well as the majority in 49 of the 50 states – cast my ballot for the 'Great Communicator', and re-elected President Ronald Reagan. Even in the often dog-eat-dog political arena, people seemed uncommonly unified.

When I arrived at college, at the State University of New York at Geneseo, the only foreshadowing of the paranormal were the annoying Ghostbusters logos taped onto the front side of each of the bedroom doors inside Erie Hall (named for the Great Lake). The movie had been very popular the summer prior, and the Residence Director must have assumed that it would be recognized as a point of cohesiveness and good humor. I thought that the movie was dreadfully inane, and I wanted to tear the offensive reminder (with a red 'ban' bar running across the childish cartoon image of a worried ghost) off of the door to my room, C2D1. I was encouraged not to by my suitemates. My roommate in room C2D1 was a student-athlete like myself named Paul. Perhaps by design, we were the same height, the same weight, and shared many similar interests. We spent so much time together in the first few weeks of the semester that our suitemates began calling us 'The Twins'. The only thing that seems to separate us were our complexions. As such I was referred to as 'The Light Twin' due to my blond hair and blue eyes, and Paul as 'The Dark Twin' as he possessed matching dark brown eyes and hair.

The beginning of that academic year stands out in my mind - to this day – as one of the most joyous and meaningful times of my life: I represented my college and state at the NCAA Regional Cross Country Championships and had lowered my 10k (6.2 miles) time down to 33:59; I had my first cartoon strip published in the college newspaper; I won election to the Dorm Council; and I spent many of free hours jumping about my room, happily lip-syncing to the latest Billy Idol CD with a black Sharpie magic marker serving as my makeshift microphone. And while I had a strong, tight-knit, group of friends in Erie Hall (male and female alike) I avoided the wild college parties, and all drinking and drugs often associated with them. My motto and philosophy, at that time, was borrowed from the great Japanese marathon runner Toshihiko Seko: "The marathon is my girlfriend, to her I give everything." My desire was to become a world-class marathon runner, and having already completed nine marathons as a teenager, I was determined that very little was going to stand in my way of that goal. I preferred the outdoors, hiking to local waterfalls and forestlands where my friends would often catch me running from tree-to-tree, and across golden fields, in my youthful birthday suit, wearing only a giant smile on my face: Life was good.

Life was good ... until Wednesday, January 30th, 1985; the cold, clear, evening that the 'demonologists', named the Warrens, rolled quietly into town. The college often brought in guest lecturers to address the student body, and on this night, it happened to be Ed and Lorraine Warren (of the Amityville Horror, The Conjuring and A Haunting in Connecticut fame). I had never heard of the Warrens, but one of my suitemates,

J. Jeff Ungar, certainly had. He invited me to accompany him to hear them speak. The event was a free one, so I eventually acquiesced and decided to join him.

Following an audio visual-laden presentation, which contained references to supposedly famous apparitions and locations such as the Brown Lady of Raynham Hall and the Jackson Homestead, members of the audience were invited to move to the front of the auditorium and greet them in person. As I stepped up to share my admiration for what turned out to be an entertaining (though, to my mind, not a 100% persuasive) demonstration, Lorraine, raised a palm towards me and refused to shake my hand, stating: "I don't want to know my future." I was summarily dismissed from the area.

My hopes that this was some misidentification, some isolated incident, vanished abruptly when twelve days later, on February 11th, 1985, I began to hear someone, or rather something, whispering my name inside my college room as I worked on a term paper; "Chrissssssssss". It sounded, at first, as though someone was talking to me from the other side of the bedroom door. No one was there. As it continued I speculated that it might be someone calling me from outside my window, from the sidewalk two stories below. No one was down there either. Returning to my seat I decided that the best course of action was to ignore whoever, or whatever, it was.

Accordingly, I switched on Paul's stereo system, placed the large headphones over my ears, and blasted "I Can't Drive 55" from Sammy Haggar's Voice of America CD. During the second refrain, inside the headphones and louder than the song, I heard it again: "Chrissssssssss".

Throwing the headphones down onto the brown, carpeted, floor of the room, I ran out of the room. "This is impossible"; I counseled myself as I sprinted (with legs that had recently run a 4:27 mile) my way down the hallway to what I hoped was safety. I wondered if Ed and Lorraine Warren actually were onto something with their research.

Several hours later, following a winter track workout at the college athletic center, I returned to room C2D1, having regained my composure. I turned the power to the stereo off, returned the headphones to their normal location and headed off across the hallway to take a well-deserved shower. I couldn't. The fact that I had showered – sometimes twice a day – often with dozens of other athletes present, did not prevent an illogical fear from washing over me. For the first time, I was afraid. I was afraid that if the water ran over my eyes, that I would not see any potential threat; and if the water ran over my ears, that I would not hear any potential threat.

That I could not attribute this fear to any particular image or experience did not comfort me. I wondered if hearing the strange, whispering, voice was the cause. Though the logical side of my brain continued to assume that it must have been some type of college prank or a misunderstanding of some easily explained situation; I was afraid. I stood, shivering, in the lone shower stall for a good twenty minutes before an opportunity finally presented itself: Paul.

I heard my roommate whistling a tune from beyond the wooden bathroom door, as he made his way through the hallway towards our shared room. My plan was a simple one: invite him into the bathroom for some type of pressing discussion, thus providing me – unbeknownst to him - with a guard.

I never got the chance.

Mere seconds after Paul entered room C2D1, he began to scream: "Holy Shit! Holy Shit!"

The intensity of his shouts unnerved me, and I took a step backward, further into the chilled shower stall. I glanced down at my shivering bare feet that now partially covered the shower drain and I hoped that I was ready for whatever it was that came next. It was Paul. He threw open the bathroom door, placed his palms down onto his jean-covered, bending, knees and he gasped loudly for air. His eyes were open wide and his chest was heaving. I pushed aside the flimsy shower curtain and called his name, which startled him.

"What's the matter with you? Why are you trying to scare the crap out of me?"

I apologized. When I asked Paul what happened, he replied only that I wouldn't believe him, and that he wanted to catch his breath and remain in the bathroom for a few minutes.

I had my guard.

When we returned to our room, I again asked Paul what happened, and after again stating that I 'wouldn't believe' him, he said it was "some crazy shit." I tried to calm my growing sense of fear as he explained that he had heard someone call my name, "Chrissssssssss", mere inches from his head, but that the room was completely empty! "I heard it twice, clear as day, and there was no one in here!" he exclaimed.

Fearing that mass hysteria might quickly ensue, I opted to say nothing about my frighteningly similar experience just a few hours earlier. Trying to wrap my mind around the strange occurrences, I deduced that there might actually be several 'logical' explanations, even if they weren't comforting ones: A possible gas leak in the room; someone potentially spiking our food or drinks with drugs; seasonal affective disorder (SAD); or perhaps the 'hissing' of aging heat pipes.

My quick, and unemotional, response to Paul: "That's weird."

The following evening, February 12th, 1985, I would learn what weird really was. Paul, having only moments before claimed that he was seeing 'shadows' over his head as he tried to study, opted to go out for the evening when he realized it was not me who was making them.

"Things are too (expletive) crazy in here right now," he protested.

So, I sat alone at my desk, eating some cinnamon-flavored candies, reading a letter that my 82-year-old great-grandmother had recently mailed to me. In it, she advised me to 'sleep well' and to 'stay warm'.

Reading the letter brought back a series of meaningful childhood memories: memories of family picnics, baseball games, homemade Italian Wedding Bell soup and rose gardens, her rose gardens. As I place the letter down on my desk, a tear in the corner of my eye, I decide to offer the person - who was now standing over my right shoulder - a piece of candy.

That was the moment that my life changed.

The SyFy show (School Spirits: Dorm Room Nightmare); the movies (Please Talk With Me; K2 Killaz; the Veil Principle); the books (Surviving Evidence; Please Talk With Me; Lost Whispers); the Coast to Coast AM appearance; the multitude of conventions and speaking engagements a quarter century later; all have their origin in that singular moment: the moment that I first saw the ghost … and in J. Jeff Ungar's enlightened decision to record it.

The 'thing' looked human, like a young male, not much older – or younger – than I was. Were it not for the fact that its legs were passing inside and through the stereo, I might have thought it was a person who had – somehow – broken into my room without me noticing him. That is until I noticed that the head seemed unconnected to the body, and then the tilted neck, and then the …

I ran, screaming, out into the college hallway, banging on the first door that I came to Jeff's. My primary concern, as a nationally-ranked athlete, was not so much the appearance of the thing, but the fact that I panicked when I did see it. Just as when a horse breaks stride in a race, if an athlete panics, the game is over.

I had panicked.

It took Jeff quite some time to calm me down enough for me to explain what had happened, other than the fact that I had panicked: I had seen a ghost! I was fortunate that Jeff, like many other children of the 1970's, enjoyed watching shows like "In Search of" and had a strong curiosity about the universe and what mysteries it might hold. Rather than shoo me away under the assumption I was under the influence (which he knew would have been out of character for me), he was curious as to what it was that I actually had seen. He wanted to see, to experience, to record, perhaps even, to understand! Following a quick visit to my room, Jeff began the process of recording my testimony, of jotting down discovered or captured evidence, and making note of other eyewitness accounts, in what would, some twenty-five years later, become known as the C2D1 Journal Notes.

The following morning, while I was at class, Jeff interviewed Paul who verified his experiences regarding the disembodied voice and the circling shadows. The detail that Paul and I had heard the whispering voice independently, and without any prior discussion or any shared knowledge, intrigued Jeff. The next night, without me sharing what I had seen on February 12th, Paul claimed that he saw a person 'with a tilted head' staring at him in the middle of the night. For Jeff it was additional confirmation that something 'real' was occurring; something that merited further investigation.

Two days later, Valentine's Day, at approximately 8 PM, Jeff and I entered C2D1; our goal was to attempt to capture the spirit on film. Jeff, with his trusty 35mm camera in hand, had been unnerved by the fact that Paul and I had gone to see a priest earlier that day, in the attempt to rid ourselves of the ghost. His reasoning was that if the ghost was trying to communicate with me (as it had continued to call my name) that there must be a purpose for it, and if we allowed ourselves the time and opportunity to do so, we might be able to learn not only who it was, but be able to ask for details about the afterlife and better understand the validity – or lack thereof - of many of the world's great religions.

For my part, I wanted it gone. The night before I had wrestled with this – thing – for the possession of my pillow, causing Paul to remark as he watched from his own bed: "No one should ever have to see what I am seeing", as I pulled with all my might, wrapping my toes around the base of my mattress, against an unseen being, for control of my pillow, which was literally hovering in mid-air. The night before, I felt its ice cold fingers rubbing the bottom of my feet as I tried to fall asleep. The night before I had seen an eerily smiling face protruding from my wall just inches from my face. I wanted it gone, and as far as I was concerned, the sooner the better.

After reading Jeff's journal entries and speaking face-to-face with both Paul and me, the priest, Fr. Charlie Manning, who worked at the Newman Interfaith Center on the college campus, had agreed to help us. He would be arriving in just three days, and Jeff wanted to make sure that we documented as much as we could prior to that occurrence.

As we entered the room, Jeff instructed me to 'call' the ghost. The thought seemed ludicrous to me on several levels, the first being that there was probably nothing that I desired less than that, and the second that I had absolutely no idea how to go about doing so. When I explained to Jeff that I had no clue how to comply with his request, he directed me to use the ghost's name in order to increase the chance that the ghost might respond to our attempt.

"I don't know its name," I protested, "I see it, I scream, I throw things at it, and then I run!"

Not to be deterred, Jeff advised that I 'feel' for a name, that I select a name that 'seems right'. Having no reliable means of doing so, I simply selected the name of a small, blue-feathered, parakeet that my family purchased when I was a small child: "Tommy".

Jeff stood motionless, seemingly stunned when I said it.

"What did you say?" he asked, eyes widening behind his thin, silver-rimmed glasses.

"Tommy. Why?"

Jeff then asked me if Paul had told me to use that name, to call the ghost 'Tommy'. Confused by this line of inquiry, I replied that Paul and I had never spoken about what the ghost's name might be, and asked him why he was so intrigued by the name that I selected. Jeff's reply sent a cold chill up my spine: "When I asked Paul if he had to give the ghost a name, what it would be, he said, 'Tommy'.

Fear.

Refocusing, Jeff instructed me to kneel on the floor, and to stretch my arms out in front of me – palms up – and to use the name I had just selected. Nervously, I did so. Jeff began taking room temperature readings using what looked to be one of those floating fish tank thermometers.

I did not have to wait long before the closet door, which I was facing as I knelt, unlatched, and opened of its own volition. A crisp, frozen, air washed out across my face, my neck, and my arms. I recognized at that moment – while Jeff diligently scribbled away in his notebook – that I didn't want to be there, that I shouldn't be there, and that if I were truly wise, I would be anywhere else.

To read more about the 'C2D1 Haunting', pick up a copy of Surviving Evidence: Memoir of an Extreme Haunting, by Christopher DiCesare (Dark Moon Press, 2014); available at Amazon.com; barnesandnoble.com and darkmoonpress.com. The award-winning (Best Feature, Spirit Film Fest; Best Director, Wilson Horror Film Fest) docu-thriller, Please Talk with Me, which recreates the events of 1985, can be purchased at ptwmthefilm.com.

The INVITATION of ASH

By Rick Kueber

I struggled to come to my senses. Something had awakened me from a sound sleep and I depressed the home-screen button on my phone... 3 am to the minute. My lazy dog Jobi was sound asleep on the bed at my feet. I started to doze again when I heard three knocks at my bedroom door. I jumped from my bed, assuming that my fourteen-year-old son must be at my door, which could only mean one of two things... he was sick to his stomach or was having another migraine. I opened the door, but he was not there. I checked the bathroom door, the computer room door and finally his room where I found him lying in bed. "Are you okay?" I asked but received no reply. "Did you knock on my door?" Again, no response.

He was sound asleep and did not even stir when I spoke, but I am getting ahead of myself. This story begins over five years ago, shortly after I had formed a paranormal research team that I cleverly named Evansville Vanderburgh Paranormal Investigations or E.V.P. investigations. We were a small team, a tight-knit family, and had only just begun when we had an unusual and amazing case involving a child who was tragically killed in an intentional fire. Her name was Ashley Sue and she had been nicknamed The Burning Girl. Ashley Sue had a reputation for visiting every team member in the most terrifying ways during our investigation, and on a rare occasion when we had wrapped up and moved on to our next adventure.

The tragic tale was so overwhelming, so heartbreaking and so important on a profound level that I felt the need to write it down, to share it with the world. On a warm and stormy evening, as I lay awake in bed, I began to peck away at the keyboard of my laptop. I'm not sure if it was a combination of the perfect sultry night and the intensity of the story that was stuck in my head or if my thoughts were guided by another force, but the words came easily. I wrote for hours and after a short sleep, I continued to write the next day. The storms outside raged on and as I approached page fifty of what was intended to be a short story, I scanned back over my work and felt a sense of pride in my accomplishment.

I continued on typing away as the story told itself. Something was amiss and I suddenly caught a scent that concerned me. A faint hot, mechanical odor drifted up and I thought perhaps I may need to give my trusty laptop a break. Unfortunately, it was not that simple. The base of my computer grew uncomfortably hot against my legs and wisps of smoke escaped from its vents. Lightning struck close and loud, rattling the windows and causing me to flinch with surprise. My screen flickered black and I could have sworn I heard the sound of a giggling child when it went completely black and shut itself down completely. In the words of the computer guru who opened it up to assess the problem, "I can't say I've ever seen anything like this before. Looks like it literally burned up from the inside out." I had not saved my work to a flash drive and was utterly distressed at the loss. I thought about writing the story again on one of the team's desktop computers but all I could do was stare at the blank screen knowing I could never rewrite the story as fluidly as I had originally. A voice inside my head told me that this had happened for a reason and now was not the time for the world to know her story.

Flash forward four years and I suddenly felt an urgency to write her story again. I took more time to write the story exactly how it felt, not just in a clinical dialogue or documentary style, but with all of the feelings of the experience and all of the ideas and possible explanations that had occurred to me in the years since. As the months passed, and the short story grew into a full-length novel I began to see a pattern. Whenever I would be deep in my writing, and the tale flowed from my fingertips like honey from a spoon, smooth, sweet and thick, I would be accompanied by a rogue electrical storm. The terrible thunderous roar and frequently brilliant flashes of lightning were inspirational in the way that it transported me back to the days when we first encountered Ashley Sue, the burning girl, the lightning rider... the most powerful entity we had ever encountered.

My manuscript in total was nearly two hundred pages and I submitted it as a self-published work and much to my surprise, people began to buy and read my book. It became a buzz on social media and I did the expected book launch party, book signings, and seminars. Each event was accompanied by an intense though sometimes short-lived, thunderstorm. Even my first radio appearance after the book's release had its own stormy visitation. The radio show publicist Annette soon befriended me and wanted to know more about my story and my book in order to acquire more radio interviews for me. Out of courtesy, I mailed her a copy of my book.

It was a sunny August day when a package arrived at Annette's home. Her daughter brought the small package into her office, but Annette was busy finishing up some business on her computer. When she had finished, she picked up the package and began to open it. A smile crossed her face when she realized the contents of the priority envelope was the book she was anticipating. While looking over the cover, the table of contents and reading the foreword, her intrigue grew. Diving into the first chapter, she quickly became caught up in the story, but before she could finish chapter two, she began to have difficulty reading in the dimming light of her office. She took her book and her drink to the backyard to read in the bright daylight, but the sky had grown overcast.

Annette sat on the back steps and read for a bit, and eventually moved herself to the rarely used trampoline where she laid down and submerged herself in the book, Forever ASH. Certain moments in the book tugged at her heart, or chilled her soul with fright and when she reached one of these moments, the wind picked up, or she would notice the sky darken even more. Reaching a chapter titled "The Lightening Rider", Annette was startled by a sudden clap of thunder. Almost immediately the sky grew ominously dark and the wind began to howl relentlessly. Taking her book inside, she curled up in a cozy blanket and continued to read by lamplight. A wailing siren snapped Annette back from the world inside the pages of her book and her daughter burst into the room.

"We have a severe storm warning!" She paced the room and peeked out of the window. "We're supposed to seek shelter."

"It's going to be fine," Annette assured her though she was a bit intimidated by the unexpected and extreme weather. "I'm just going to sit here and read a while longer."

The moment the words left Annette's lips, a massive bolt of lightning struck nearby filling their ears with a painful crashing noise and immediately, the house went dark. With that obvious warning, Annette took shelter with the rest of her family as the frightening gale battered their home and small community. As suddenly and unexpectedly as it had arrived, the storm dissipated and the sky cleared.

Annette had not made a connection between the storm and the book until the next day when we spoke. I was explaining a theory about the little lightening rider and all of the experiences that had accompanied the book events. We talked at length about the numerous incidents surrounding the book events and how much she was enjoying the book.

"Oh, that reminds me..." She began. "I was really getting into the book yesterday when out of nowhere we had this really scary storm blow in. It was a beautiful day and then all of the sudden, it was like 'CRASH' with wind and torrential rain and thunder and lightning... and then we lost power and I had to stop reading."

I spoke only two words, but they shook Annette and chilled her very soul. "She knows."

"Wait... what do you mean, she knows?" She knew the answer but hoped I would give another explanation.

"I mean, Ashley knows you are reading the book and she likes to make herself known when her story is being told..." I wasn't trying to frighten her. I was only being honest. "I think you had a visitor last night. Now that she knows you, she may continue to visit at times, but she isn't malicious... anymore."

Later that week, as my book began to sell quite well, instant messages, emails, text messages and social media posts began flooding in.

A very good friend of the team, Amanda, had helped us on a few investigations with research and came along during our investigating of 'The Haunting of the Owls' (which I wrote my second book about). It was late one afternoon when I received a text message from Amanda saying she had stayed up all night reading the book and when she had finished, she had the most frightening nightmares.

"It was like I was in the book. I had the craziest, most vivid dreams I   think I've ever had!" ~Amanda
"Wow! Sorry..."~Rick
"What are you sorry about? It's been a long time since a book or movie   gave me nightmares. Just means it's a great book."~Amanda
"I said sorry 'cause it might not have just been a dream. Sometimes Ashley likes to visit people when they tell the story or read the book.   I'm afraid I may have just unleashed a haunting on dozens, maybe hundreds of unsuspecting people."~Rick
"That's actually pretty awesome! :)"~Amanda
"Thanks, but I don't think everyone is going to feel the same way as you do."~Rick

The conversation continued off and on for days. Amanda was such an enthusiast; she actually reread the book several times just to have visits and encounters with the little burning girl. It was in the midst of one of our message conversations that I received a message on a social media site that I frequented.

"Rick, I have just read your book 'Forever ASH' on my Kindle. I was so moved by the story that it felt like the little girl was there with me as I read. I could picture her and even thought I saw her one night when I woke during a storm. It felt so real, so personal... It was heartbreakingly beautiful."
Deanna, United Kingdom

30

Emails and messages of this type trickled in and many people spoke up at seminars and book signings saying they had experienced similar things. I was beginning to get comfortable with hearing these stories and I was actually relieved that almost everyone was excited about their experiences. It didn't hurt my feelings that I had not been having visits for a while. I had started to think my visitations from Ashley were ending.

Annette and I had become good friends while she read the book. In fact, I began reading it again and though we were hundreds of miles apart, we read the book together... sending each other messages about where we were, or what part she had really been engrossed by. We were in the midst of one of these text and reading evenings when she messaged me.

"Hang on... somebody's at the door."~Annette
"OK. I'll be here."~Rick
"Well, that was weird. Nobody was there."~Annette
"No one you could see, anyway, huh? Lol!"~Rick
"Quit it!"~Annette

I continued to receive messages and comments about countless experiences surrounding the book and its story. Weeks passed and Annette had traveled to Springfield, IL. She called me upon their arrival to tell me of yet another interesting 'coincidence'.

"So... we were headed down the interstate, on our way to Springfield IL... I was sitting in the back and had been telling everyone about this creepy book I had just read. When we stopped at a gas station, my friends got out to fill up the tank and grab something to drink. One of them asked if I wanted anything. I said, 'yeah. Grab me a coke.' When she came back and we were about to get back on the road, she handed me the bottle of coke. I said, 'Holy hell!' and they were both like, 'what!?!?' I turned the bottle around to show them the saying on the side of the bottle that said, 'Share a Coke with Ashley'. They were like, 'yeah... so?' and I said 'You remember the book I was talking about and the storms and everything? Well, the girl's name was Ashley.' I swear their jaws dropped to the floor!" Annette laughed.

"Holy crap! That's an awesome story!" I couldn't wait to retell it at my next event.

"Oh and that's not all." She continued.

"There's more? Don't leave me hanging!" I joked.

"It was a nice, sunny day when we left and after we left the gas station the sky kept getting darker and darker and we ran into one hell of a storm. It was so bad we actually had to pull over because we couldn't even see the road!" I could feel the anxiety in her voice. "But it finally let up and we did make it."

"That is one hell of a story!" I would have given anything to have been in the car for that trip. The stories continued to flow in and I continued to share them whenever I had a public event or radio show. My writing went on to produce two more books to finish out my trilogy, but while I wrote and went about my life and my team's investigations, my readers were not the only ones having experiences.

***

I suppose this brings us back to the beginning of my story and the first of many late night interludes, like the 3 am knocks on my bedroom door.

***

I was stuck in the middle of a chapter in my second book. It wasn't that I didn't know what I needed to say. I was having a difficult time putting the frighteningly eerie feeling of having such an intense and personal paranormal encounter into words. I did not want the truth of it to get lost in translation.

"CRASH!" A loud noise came from the other end of my three bedroom apartment. I jumped up and ran into the hallway, assuming that my son had dropped or broken something. I darted down the hall and stopped short when my son called out from his computer desk, which was in the room next to mine.

"What was that?" He said loudly as I scurried by.
"I don't know. I thought it was you." I said honestly.

"Nope. Not me." was all he said and turned his attention back to his computer screen.

I looked around his room, the kitchen and then the dining and living rooms. I found nothing out of order and decided to sink into the sofa and rest my brain. Perhaps that was all I needed to get just the right words to describe that unnerving memory. I stared blankly across the room when I suddenly noticed something very odd. A thick framed piece of art that had hung on the wall near my flat screen television was sitting on the floor and leaning against the wall. The hook was still in its place on the wall and the frame wire was still attached to the frame of the artwork. The bottom corner of the frame was busted from the fall, but it did not add up at all. Somehow the piece had raised up over the hook and hit the floor hard enough to break the frame, but still remain upright. A chill ran the length of my spine and my hair stood on end.

"Thanks," I said politely to the empty room and quickly dove back into my novel, remembering exactly how to describe the feeling of ghostly terror.

A few nights later, I was up late writing when three knocks came to my bedroom door again. I called out, 'Yes?' but got no response. Again no one was there, and the dog and my boy were sound asleep.

Days and weeks passed and I was frequently awakened by a knocking at my bedroom door. I was disturbed by the phenomenon and by my lack of uninterrupted sleep. I began to think back on all of the odd incidents that I had experienced in my own home and recalled Annette telling me of having a knocking at her office door when she read my book, 'Forever ASH'. So I had a thought... Later that week, when I was in the middle of writing, I was interrupted by a knock at my door. I opened it up wide and spoke.

"Ashley, if you are here, you are welcome to come in as long as you mean no harm. I will be your friend and if you remain peaceful and quiet, you will always have an open invitation here." I stood there and held the door with one hand and held my other arm out in a welcoming fashion. I typed away in the silent room and the scent of warm vanilla began to fill the air. I looked up from my keyboard and glanced around the room to find a scented jar candle on my entertainment center lit, its dim yellow glow flickered and caused shadows to dance on the walls.

"That smells nice Ashley, but you shouldn't do that... It could be dangerous." I said kindly and offered a sad smile. "I'd hate to have a fire and have something bad happen with my son only a few rooms away."

I left the candle burning while I wrote and listened as a storm began to brew outside my window. In the midst of typing my latest book, I paused at times to acknowledge the presence of my spectral friend. "I'm glad you came to visit again." and "My friends have been telling me about your visits. I hope you aren't frightening them too much." We're among my conversation with the invisible and ethereal spirit child. Ashley continues to visit me, my team and many random readers, though the stories have quieted down some. Her spirit no longer haunts, but merely pays visits. She has found her peace through the revelation of her story, Forever ASH.

Rick Kueber is the author of the Frost and Flame Trilogy based on real cases by EVP Investigations in Evansville, Indiana. The books are "Forever Ash; The Witch Child of Helmach Creek," "Shadows of Eternity: The Children of the Owls," and "Neverending Maddness: A Girl Lost to the World." (sic)
Rick is also author of a Science Fiction Serial, The Convergence Saga, book 1 "The Pale Titan" and book 2 "The Genesis Project."
Rick Kueber author page on Amazon

The Black Eyed People

By Annette Munnich

For five years, whenever I tried to tell these stories I would begin to tremble.

I was the host of Python Radio for 4 years beginning in 2007. I started in radio by accident having been a news person on a friend's show. We were broadcast over the internet from a station in South Carolina. Over time, there was a dispute with the show host and the owner of the station and everyone connected to that show was terminated except for me.

At that point, I was encouraged to host my own show but I felt I wasn't ready for it. It took six months for me to be ready to do this. The reasoning was that I was not ego motivated but felt that through the guests I would interview I might attain some answers to my own questions about what had happened in my life. I never told this particular story on air which is at the heart of what frankly scared me shitless.

I have had paranormal experiences since I was 16. These include seeing spirit, being touched my spirit, and dreams that were prophetic, Deja Vu experiences, and dreams that I am convinced were spirit communication.

I have a theory that over time our abilities get stronger due to more and more sensitivity towards the spirit world plus I believe they can tell that people like me are more likely to see them, feel them etc... so they are drawn to that energy coming from us. They know. We become beacons for it I think. I coined the phrase passive medium for it because there are a lot of us who do not try to contact the dead and yet they find us.

The Creepy Kid

The creepy kid would walk by my house sometimes and I worked with him. We (my husband, our four children and me) had moved into this big old house that was a very good price just outside the Chicago city limits. It would unnerve me a bit when he walked by and the way he looked at the place. Maybe he was looking for me. I think he had a crush on me as we had become very close.

I worked as a waitress part-time at night and he was a busboy. I think he was 17 and still in High School thought not doing well. I started talking to him one day because I saw him sketching and he was a brilliant artist though his drawings were full of horror and sadness. Startling, actually, sometimes with the darkness they portrayed.

Somehow I can't remember his name though I recall his face very well. He had shoulder-length black hair and big dark eyes but pale like a character in a Tim Burton movie. It turned out that we had the same birthday and shared a passion for art and he and I would talk when we weren't busy.

We had paranormal activity in our new home from the very beginning which wasn't so new for me. I do also think that sometimes the right person shows up at the right place and it triggers the perfect storm however in this instance I should say the wrong person shows up at the wrong place...

The creepy kid was one of the people who told me that the house was previously occupied by devil worshipers. This information had also been told to me by two separate neighbors with details about rituals in the backyard and the original owner carrying his mother out of the home dead with a garbage bag over her head and drove her to the funeral home when she passed away there. I had found a secret ritual room in the basement and the attic had strange symbols written on the walls. The bedroom my husband and I shared had black walls and ceiling plus red wax in the carpeting. It took seven coats of paint to get rid of the black walls.

I was telling him along the way about the strange things that went on in the home.

I asked about his artwork and the macabre and chilling subject matter he was choosing constantly and he told me that he was in a satanic cult that he couldn't get out of. He told me he tried to quit and they cursed his eyes. I didn't really know what that meant. He was enormously upset about it and very insistent. That day as he looked about to cry he rolled up his sleeves and I saw the healed over cutting scars from his wrists to his inner elbows on both arms. I really was concerned and praying a lot for this guy now.

I felt like I had darkness surrounding me at home and at work. There was an unreal quality to it all.

One night he left early before his job was done and the next day they fired him with me standing right there. He looked at me and said why don't you stick up for me and ask them to let me keep my job?" He looked at me with hurt in his eyes and said, "I curse you."

I was pregnant and had only found out a few weeks before this.

The Home

The home was a craftsman style bungalow with a nice porch and the beautiful little stained glass windows. We had a two car garage that also had a porch attached. I liked this house. It felt sad. No amount of painting and TLC seemed to lift the shroud of heaviness that could be felt there. The main floor and upstairs were sad but the basement was alive with an angry energy that felt electric and terrifying. I had to mentally psych myself up to go down there to do laundry and each time I ended up running up the stairs as fast as I could feeling like something was directly behind me. The ritual room was down there and I did manage to clean it up; removing the condoms, syringes, and other items I found as well as getting the walls back to a benign white.

The toys in the kid's room on the first floor moved by themselves and my oldest son saw a jacket walking across the backyard with no person inside of it. We had bugs and Orkin came time and time again telling me I could not possibly still have any insects and yet we did.

My mother came from California and stayed three nights. After that, she would stay at my brother's house because she said all the alarm clocks and radios would go off simultaneously at 3 am and she couldn't turn them off. She said it was blaring loud and yet we didn't wake up. She was afraid.

The yard was barren except for some patchy grass. I normally have a green thumb but everything I planted there died even bulbs and bushes.

We bought a Virgin Mary statue to put in the front yard. It faced the street. Over time, we began to joke that we should turn ours around so it would face the house.

I had crucifixes and angels and holy water fonts. I thought everything there could be lightened up and brought back to goodness. The house began to focus its attention on me alone. I was the antagonist by my mere presence. Me and my religious stuff. On the day before Halloween traditionally called Devil's Night, I was up early making treats for the kid's Halloween parties that day at school when I had a severe pain. My baby was due in December. The pain was below my ribcage on the left side. I tried to lie down but couldn't sleep. The treats would never make it to the party. My husband took me to the ER. The doctors did not know what was wrong with me so I was under observation. At about 4 pm I sat up and threw up, then passed out and went into shock. I was in and out of consciousness with doctors and nurses hurriedly rushing me to the delivery room for an emergency cesarean section.

When the doctor made the incision blood began pouring out of me like a faucet. I was hemorrhaging and no one knew from where or why. My daughter had a cleft lip and was six weeks premature. They told my husband that I might not make it.

A scope was used and when blood squirted on it, they found the torn artery. My chest muscle had ripped. The doctor was able to repair it and I was given three pints of blood.

Baby and I had an extended stay at the hospital when we went home a mistake in dosage directions of her medication caused her to lose weight and sleep almost all the time. We went back to the hospital and she was there for 4 more days. I was told she could have died. They took the medicine bottle and never gave it back to me. I remember sitting in a rocking chair in the nursery at the hospital for hours holding Bri and looking out the windows at the tops of the autumn trees that still had some splashes of gold and russet leaves. We had each other and we had some peace.

In February, my husband had a stroke and was paralyzed on the left side of his body. He was 35.

He recovered after months of painful physical therapy. In March, we had surgery for our daughter's cleft lip at the University of Chicago and it was repaired beautifully.

Amidst all of this we had checks lost in the mail, the car breaking down, things lost only to turn up in unlikely places. I feel that we were under demonic oppression which is not possession but is being surrounded by an evil that harasses the people involved tirelessly and without mercy in many different ways.

Black Eyed People

We lived in this house for two years. People always ask why a person would stay in a situation like this but it cost so much to move in and fix it up. The oppression and health problems made it difficult to get ahead much after that. The size of our family made it impossible that we could just move in with relatives. Also scary things did not happen every day, thank God.

In November of 1996, Cardinal Joseph Bernardin of Chicago died from pancreatic cancer. There was a friendship between him and my great aunt who was a Mother Superior in Cincinnati from the time that he was Archbishop there. The wake (viewing) for him was at Holy Name

Cathedral downtown and it was around the clock 24 hours a day. So I went.

It was later in the evening and a very cold night. The line to the doors at Holy Name was about 6 blocks long. The sidewalks downtown are very wide so it was just a ton of people.

There was an older man behind me and he made some light conversation about baseball. He seemed very friendly and nice. He seemed a decent average guy bundled up for the weather with gray hair and glasses maybe sixty-five years old as a guess.

What happened next has scarred me for life and instilled a fear of crowds that I am unable to get over. I never realized how vulnerable a person is in a loud, thick crowd.

As this man and I were talking he looked at my face and his whole face changed in a way that was slightly contorted with his eyes turning black. He hated me and wanted to do me harm. I turned around facing forward again and stopped talking. The man pressed himself up against my back and was touching me. I could feel his hot breath in my ear as he began growling like an animal. I tried pushing my way through the crowd away from him and managed to get a little bit ahead of him with some people separating us. I could feel him back there staring at me but I did not have the courage to look.

Less than 10 minutes later I reached the steps to the Cathedral which caused the crowd entering the church to turn to the left. On the steps, I turned to look at him and his eyes were still black and fixated on me totally in a hateful way. It was the way a wolf might follow a rabbit with its eyes and all of its senses. I quickly found a pew near a lot of people where I could pray and watch the door. I was shaking.

That man never entered the church.

I had never had a situation where paranormal occurrences started following me around in the world wherever I went so I felt very shaken and vulnerable. Whatever was in this house was able to make my life hell at any time. I cannot begin to describe how that felt. I believe it chose the wake to prove a point that even outside a church with a throng of mourners it could touch me.

I began looking for some help with this situation and through a friend I was introduced to a Native American Spirit Woman. I was very thankful to have someone to consult with me. This woman was my friend's grandmother's friend. This is what she told me. She taught me to draw a circle with myself and family members inside and all dark forces outside of the circle with the line protected by God. The woman told me that evil spirits can enter the bodies of others and leave a short while later without the person ever realizing that they have lost a small amount of time. She told me that some people are more vulnerable to this than others for the reasons of their lack of morality, mental illness or willingly giving up part of their consciousness to substance abuse.

I was instructed to ignore these people when I saw them and show no reaction as the fear made them stronger. I was reminded that I was protected by my faith from serious harm and that this was a game of sorts. A game I didn't want to play for sure but here I was.

I was at my waitress job when a customer walked in and turned to look at me while he was standing in line. When he saw me his face hardened and his eyes turned black as he fixated on me. No one seemed to see this but me. Everything was continuing normally around him. I went into the ladies room and stayed there for 20 minutes. When I came out he was gone. This man was a lot taller and younger than the older man in the church line. He looked very intimidating. It was hard not to be startled and react.

We moved out of the house into a smaller place 30 miles away. I didn't want to leave the area we were in but I was more than happy to say goodbye to the home we suffered so much in. This new house did not have paranormal activity which was a very sweet thing for all of us.

I walked through the living room while we were still in the first few days of unpacking and noticed a man standing on the sidewalk looking at me. He had black eyes and a hateful stare. I walked into the kitchen acting as if I had not noticed him. Maybe ten minutes later I walked through the room and saw that he was still there intently looking at the living room from the sidewalk about 15 feet away from the glass window. He was frozen in that pose and in that spot like a statue.

A little while later I saw that he was gone. I feel this was a calling card from my old home saying we know where you went.

Annette Munnich is the owner of Stellium Books *and the author of* 9 Angels for Prosperity and Abundance *and* Ghost Journal & Record Book.

The Malevolent Schoolmaster Specter

By Paranormal Investigator and Author Joni Mayhan

I had a bad feeling as I led my group to the haunted dormitory building.

The sensation felt like iron butterflies in the pit of my stomach trying to break free. I glanced back at the group of people behind me, seeing the mixture of expectation and apprehension on their faces. Should I turn back now before anything bad could happen?

"Is everything okay, Joni?" one of them asked. I guarded my expression, showing them nothing more than what they needed to see. If I expressed any emotion, it would impact their experience, and the last thing I wanted to do was to make them fearful.

Fear often feeds negative entities, giving them the power to expand their abilities. If something negative was here, I certainly didn't want to fuel it up with pure nitro as we waltzed through the door.

Built in 1832, **Parsonsfield Seminary** was originally founded by the Freewill Baptists to serve as a high school for local students. It functioned for 117 years until it finally ran out of funding and was turned over to the Consolidated School Board to use for various functions. By 1986, the school board moved to another location, leaving the building empty for the first time in its 154 year history. It was then purchased by a non-profit group who wanted to preserve the location.

On paper, there was no reason why the seminary should be haunted.

If you perused through the newspapers and historical documents, you wouldn't find one anomaly to suggest foul play. There weren't any mysterious deaths, no claims of abuse and no reports of wrongdoings whatsoever. The building should have been a happy place filled with glorious memories of bygone days, but it wasn't. It's one of the most haunted locations I've ever investigated.

It took years before the people who cared for the seminary acknowledged the haunting. They were probably aware of it but found ways to turn a blind eye when they encountered anything strange. The sound of footsteps in a vacant area could be explained as squirrels on the roof. Doors that closed themselves could be attributed to air pressure inside the old building. Voices drifting on the wind could be someone's imagination. It wasn't until a contractor began doing electrical work inside the dormitory building that the full extent of the haunting was brought to light.

The man was atop a ladder, rewiring the ancient electrical system when he heard the distinct sound of his lunch bag rattling below him. When he came back down the ladder moments later, the bag was gone. He searched the building but discovered he was very much alone. After experiencing several other equally curious happenings, he contacted psychic medium Barbara Williams.

Barbara is well known in the Maine area for her exceptional mediumship skills. She teaches at a local retreat, as well as conducting private readings and investigations. She checked out the buildings and confirmed his suspicions. The seminary buildings were haunted. Over the course of the next few years, she did more studies, bringing in select investigators to research the facilities. As a favor to us, she allowed our group to come in to investigate periodically.

Being a paranormal investigator and author, I've been to some amazingly spooky places, including a plethora of haunted asylums and old prisons. Haunted buildings shouldn't affect me like this one did, but I couldn't shake the trepidation.

The building in front of me was called Doe Hall, named after a former administrator from the seminary's early years. Long and white, it was three stories tall with twin doorways situated at either end of the building. The dark windows twinkled in the moonlight, telling me nothing.

I thought about turning around but couldn't bring myself to do it. The people were part of a meet-up group who had paid good money for the pleasure of experiencing a paranormal investigation. I was supposed to be their group leader. They trusted me to be fearless and brave, not someone who ran away at the first sign of trouble. I took a deep cleansing breath, said a prayer and then moved on.

"Ready or not, here we come," I whispered under my breath.

I pushed open the door and felt the dead air caress my face. It smelled stagnant and stale, like air trapped inside a coffin. It wasn't difficult to imagine the souls of the dead whisking through the room, creeping closer to check us out. I repressed a shudder and crossed the foyer.

The interior of the building was impressive. Restored to its original glory, it was like taking a step back in time. The foyer was broad and square, with four rooms and a staircase branching off it. Intricately carved woodwork graced the cornices and moldings while photos of former administrators lined the walls. Looking into their eyes reminded me of a scary Jesus picture from my childhood. No matter where I moved in the room, those eyes followed me.

We reached the mahogany staircase that would lead us to the second and third floors.

The last time I had this feeling was when I contended with the Soul Collector. For several months, I had a negative attachment that many felt was demonic. Living through that and surviving left me with symptoms that were similar to Post Traumatic Shock Disorder. If I was once the first one in a dark building, now I paused and assessed the situation. Maybe I was just reacting to the past.

"What was this building used for?" one of the men asked, startling me out of my thoughts.

Thankfully, I recovered quickly, realizing I'd been standing on the bottom stair for more than a moment. I tucked my hair behind my ear and turned with a smile.

"This was the dormitory building where the children stayed. The bottom floor is mostly administration and public areas, but the second and third floors house the dorm rooms," I said.

I climbed the stairs to the third floor, making sure the trail of people was still behind me. I listened to them chatter amicably, excited about the prospects. Most of the people in my group had never been on a ghost hunt before and were quite excited.

My long-time friend Sandy MacLeod was the meet-up coordinator and helped me with the group. Since twenty people showed up for the event, we divided them between four group leaders. She took me aside.

"Are you okay? You seem a bit preoccupied?" she asked.

I took a deep breath and let it out in a sigh. "Yeah, I'm fine. I just keep getting a bad feeling, almost like a premonition," I told her.

She studied me for a moment. "We can always investigate another building and leave this one until later," she suggested.

I noticed the others in the group watching us. "No. I'm fine. It's probably nothing."

The truth was: there was negative energy in the building. We felt it several times but it always kept its distance. I was probably just overreacting.

Our group included a woman in her late twenties named Carleen, a former Marine named Daryl and a contractor from nearby Salem named Jeff. Of the three of them, only Jeff had been on an investigation before. The others were complete newbies.

"What do you think about this, Daryl?" I asked, knowing he'd never been on an investigation before.

"I don't believe in this stuff. I'm just here because my girlfriend made me go," he told us.

Sandy and I exchanged grins. Skeptics were often the first ones to have experiences at a haunted location. It was almost like throwing down a gauntlet to them. I only hoped they were gentle with him. I finished climbing the stairs and then paused on the third-floor landing to give myself a chance to catch my breath. The air upstairs was distinctly cooler. Normally in a situation like this, the air would be warmer since heat has a tendency to rise, but this wasn't the case at the seminary. An icy chill hung in the August air as though blown into the building by an army of air conditioning units. Fluctuations in temperature, especially those as dramatic as this, were often a sign of paranormal activity. It's almost as though they suck all the warm air right out of the room.

"Okay, this is the third-floor boy's dormitory area. We've had quite a few experiences here," I told them, thinking fondly of the numerous EVPs we recorded in the past. The ghosts in this location were downright chatty, whispering into our digital recorders as though it required little effort.

Below is an EVP captured at Parsonsfield Seminary during an investigation. On it, you can hear me tell them to back off and speak to us one at a time because we were getting a rush of voices. The response is, "We're not going to behave."

https://soundcloud.com/jonimayhan/one-at-a-time-were-not-going

The hallway was long and narrow, lit only by the hazy beams of our flashlights. As I walked down it, I glanced into the dorm rooms. Thanks to the efforts of the non-profit that purchased the buildings, the rooms were being renovated and staged with furniture to make them look much like they did a hundred years ago. Most of the small rooms had beds and dressers in them.

Several had been decorated with pictures and decorative items. Sometimes, I caught sight of staring face smiling at me from a framed wall photo. I led the group all the way down the hallway to the last room on the right, the room we nicknamed "The Wheelchair Room" due to an old wheelchair that sat in the corner.

We found seats in the room and got to work. I've always had good luck with my spirit box, so I set it up in the middle of the room. As soon as I turned it on, it began scanning through the radio stations, providing white noise that the ghosts could use to communicate. We started the session by introducing ourselves and were astounded when one of the ghosts immediately responded.

After Carleen introduced herself, the spirit box said, "Hi Carleen!"

https://soundcloud.com/jonimayhan/wheelchair-room-voice-box-1

"Oh wow, that's crazy!" Jeff said.

"Are you sure that wasn't just radio interference?" Daryl asked.

"You never know, Daryl. Let's see what else we get," I told him, trying to keep the sense of aggravation out of my voice. Having a skeptic in the group was often a downer. If he was anything like the other skeptics I'd experienced, I would spend half the night defending everything we discovered.

"Maybe the ghosts will school him for us," Sandy whispered in my ear, making me smile. "We should be so lucky," I told her.

After twenty minutes in the Wheelchair Room, we moved down the hallway and checked out a few more rooms, not finding anything overly exciting. The spirit box had grown quiet, which didn't surprise me. Sometimes we tend to wear them out after a productive session.

"Let's try the girl's side of the dormitory," Sandy suggested.

I arched my eyebrows at her. "Are you sure?" I asked. The last time we were there, we felt a sense of negative energy lingering on the girl's side of the building. Barbara thought it might be a former schoolmaster.

"We'll be fine. If we run into any problems, we can always find Barbara," she said, which was reassuring. Barbara was the strongest psychic medium I knew. She could help us if we had any issues.

"Sounds like a plan," I said, trying to quiet my inner nerves.

Nothing bad was going to happen.

I chanted those words in my head as we walked back down the narrow hallway to a room I always thought of as the Gateway Room. It must have originally been used as a dormitory room, but a doorway had been cut into the other side of it, linking the boy's side to the girl's side.

When the seminary was in operation, the boys and girls were separated to prevent any hanky-panky among the students. However, when renovations were started, a small doorway was discovered in the Gateway Room's closet, allowing them secretive access to one another. It was something that usually made people chuckle. The secret doorway was only one of the mysteries surrounding the dormitory building. The other dealt with the negative energy.

Why would a seminary with such a tragedy-free history be so haunted?

After investigating there several times, I knew there was more to the buildings than what was being discussed. People of wealth and power have a great deal of affluence in their towns, especially back in the nineteenth century. It wouldn't be difficult to hide incidents from the public. After all, children back then didn't have any rights. If they talked about abuse, would anyone truly listen to them?

Suppose one of the schoolmasters had a dark hobby that required the participation of unwilling children? Where else would he work but at a facility that provided him with ample opportunities? We see it in modern days with child predators posing as scout leaders and daycare teachers. It made sense that it could have happened back then too.

Barbara Williams confirmed that something was amiss. She once left a digital recorder in the attic for an hour while she visited the schoolhouse building, which is located next door on the property. When she came back and listened to it, she was astounded. The recording included a thirty-minute account of a child pleading with someone. "Please don't hurt me," it said over and over again.

It certainly supported the theory behind the haunting. The dead often linger when they've met tragic endings. It also lent a sense of credibility to the presence of the negative entity. If someone had abused the children, the abuser might fear the repercussions he would face on the other side of the white light. Considering the location, he might have been a person of faith. If that were the case, he would have worried that his passage into the afterlife might bring him to a place of fire and brimstone instead of angels and harps. Good people went to Heaven. Bad people went to Hell. It would present a scenario where the lost souls were trapped in a never-ending hell with their abuser, repeating the history over and over again.

"Here goes nothing," I whispered to myself.

As we crossed over into the girl's dormitory area, the vibe changed immediately. The air sizzled with energy, as though thousands of souls zipped around the room. The sensation of being watched was so strong, I swiveled around several times, fully expecting to find a wayward soul watching me from the doorway of an empty room.

"It feels different over here," Jeff commented. I couldn't agree more. Was this the reason for my earlier apprehension?

I wasn't sure, but I led them to the first room I came to.

"Let's go in here," I suggested, directing the beam of my flashlight around the long narrow room.

In the center of the room was an old barber chair. It was missing a portion of the seat and couldn't be used for seating, so we pushed it against the wall and found spots surrounding it. Sandy turned on her spirit box and we began asking questions.

At first, the responses seemed to come from a child. We began structuring our questions around the child, hoping to gather more information. I especially wanted to know why he had remained earthbound, but he refused to answer. Sometimes, the best way to uncover the history of a haunted location was to ask the ghosts themselves, but they frequently wouldn't answer the questions we wanted answers to. They would tell us their favorite colors and the names of their pets, but kept the important details to themselves. It always made me wonder if there were rules on the other side. Were they not allowed to talk about some things?

"Why are we getting boys responding on the girl's side of the dormitory?" Carleen asked.

It was a good question. Logically, we should only be hearing from girls.

"Maybe they followed us over?" Sandy suggested.

"Or maybe they crawled through that secret passage in the Gateway Room," Jeff said, which made far more sense to me. We settled in, hoping for answers that would never come.

As suddenly as it began, the responses stopped. The air grew impossibly colder as a gush of energy rushed into the room, feeling like a tidal wave of negative emotion. Every hair on my arm stood at attention.

"What was that? Somebody just came in here," Jeff said. It was apparent that Jeff also possessed some mediumship abilities because he was feeling the exact same sensation I felt. Sandy must have felt it too because she directed her next question towards the new energy.

"Who just joined us? Can you tell us your name?" she asked.

Immediately a voice comes through and began spurting vile profanity.

We had been collectively leaning forward, listening intently for the response. As soon as we heard it, we simultaneously shifted backward, stunned looks on our faces.

"Did that just say what I thought it said?" Daryl asked.

"Sounded like the f-word," Jeff said. Carleen had grown very quiet. I could barely make her out in the corner of the room. If anything else happened, I knew I needed to get the group out of the room. We were slated to sleep in the dorm rooms overnight. If we had a negative experience, we were going to be in a difficult situation considering we were hours away from the nearest hotel.

"I'm not sure what I just heard, but that was unexpected. That's not very nice. Is there somebody else with us? Is a man with us now?" Sandy asked. Red-headed and often fiery, she was the mother of our group, the one who often stepped forward to take care of everyone. "If you're going to talk like that, we aren't going to continue communicating with you," she said adamantly. As though challenged, the voice on the spirit box repeated the litany of profanity.

https://soundcloud.com/jonimayhan/barber-chair-room-message

"Those aren't words they're allowed to use on the radio," Daryl commented, his voice trembling ever so slightly.

"I don't like the way this feels," Carleen added. "Me neither," I said, standing up. Every cell in my body screamed at me to get out of that room. It was so strong, I could hear the words echoing in my head. If there had been doubting before, it was long gone. This was the reason for my earlier anxiety. If I didn't get them out, something bad was going to happen. "Let's get out of here."

While Sandy retrieved her spirit box from the floor, I turned on my flashlight and picked my way around the old barber chair to the front of the room. When my fingers touched the door, a sense of panic spiked through me.

There was no doorknob on the door. "Oh my God," I whispered under my breath, trying to wedge my fingers in between the door and the frame, but it was closed tightly. The last person who came into the room must have pushed it shut, not realizing it was missing the doorknob.

As an experienced investigator, I knew to control my emotions, but there was no stopping the absolute horror that ran hot and wild through my body. The energy in the room continued to build, making the air pressure almost unbearable. It felt like we were in the heart of a tornado.

Dear God. What was happening?

Something made a tremendous crash at the far end of the room, which was followed by another pounding sound in the mad darkness on my right. Invisible fingers trailed along the bare skin on my arm, nearly sending me skyward.

"There's no doorknob!" I finally managed to say.

The others pushed against me, like a mobbing crowd.

We needed to get out now!

As another crash sounded from behind us, Daryl yanked a ring of keys out of his pocket and shoved one into the locking mechanism, trying to get the clasp to release. After a few harried seconds of fumbling fingers, the lock finally disengaged and the door swung inward. We nearly trampled one another in our efforts to leave the space.

My first instinct was based on pure survival. I wanted out. I yearned to race down the stairs, taking them two at a time, but I held myself in check. We could not flee the building.

Running away would only empower the negative entity, giving him a blueprint to work with. If he knew he could scare us, he would do it to others too. I also didn't want the group to lose their nerve. If I allowed them to flee, the only thing they would remember was the fear.

I stopped them in the hallway.

"Let's just stand here for a moment before we do anything else. The last thing we want to do is run away." I saw their pale faces staring at me from the shadows. Their eyes were wide as they moved closer.

"Why don't we just head down the hallway to another room?" Sandy suggested.

I heaved a sigh of relief. "That sounds like a great idea. Let's try the room on the end where someone smelled lilacs earlier," I suggested. I saw several nods, so I led them down another narrow hallway.

This hallway was shorter than the others, with two doorways on each side. The first two rooms were used for storage, but the room on the end to the left was staged with a bed and dresser. Earlier in the evening as we were doing a walk-through of the building another investigator had smelled lilacs. Knowing that the dead often send us scents as a sign of their presence, I took comfort in that. Anyone who would send us the smell of flowers couldn't be bad, right? I envisioned an old lady, possibly a school marm who took care of the children. I practically bolted down the hallway.

I paused in the doorway as I came to the room and shined my flashlight around it. I don't know what I was looking for. It wasn't as though the specter of an evil schoolmaster would show himself, but I wanted to make sure nonetheless. The room looked as benign as any of the other rooms.

It wasn't staged as nicely, though. The sagging bed was pushed up against the wall, the stained blue and white striped mattress bare of any dressings. A small dresser was parked just inside the doorway but was void of decorations. Several folding chairs were placed around the room, possibly placed there by another group of investigators, so we quickly took our seats.

As Sandy came in the room last, I gestured towards the spirit box in her hand.

"Why don't you turn that on and make sure he didn't follow us," I said.

"Good idea," she said.

I sat on the edge of the bed, keeping my eyes locked on the dark doorway. My senses were on heightened alert as I tried to calm down my thumping heart. If we heard the same male voice come across the spirit box, we would have no choice but to leave the building. We weren't a group of spiritual warriors. We were a mixture of newbies and budding mediums. This wouldn't be our battle to fight.

I've always been a firm believer in knowing your limitations, especially in the paranormal field. If you encounter something that wigs you out, you can stand and face it or you can find someone who is better prepared to deal with it. This was something Barbara should handle.

Sandy bent down to place the spirit box on the ground. As soon as she turned it on, the male voice blasted from the speakers, again saying the same foul words. Thankfully, I still had my digital recorder running because I captured an EVP at that moment that set my hair on end later when I listened to my audio.

The moment when Sandy bent over, the same male voice said, "Bend over."

https://soundcloud.com/jonimayhan/lilac-room-as-sandy-bent-over

I sprung to my feet.
"Let's get out of here," I said. Nobody protested as we hurried towards the door.

I led them down the stairs to the first floor, trying to keep my pace slow and steady so no one tripped and fell in their rush to vacate the building. By the time we made it to the front porch, we were running high on adrenaline.

"What was that?" Jeff asked.

"Nothing good," I said, taking a deep breath as Daryl pushed past me. The tough as nails former Marine and skeptic paused only to collect his girlfriend before he scrambled to his car, never to return. His first paranormal encounter would probably also be his last.

The rest of us found couches and cots on the second floor, spending a sleepless night staring at the shadows, waiting for the malevolent schoolmaster to find us. As dawn hovered over the horizon, it sent spears of golden light through the windows, chasing away the threatening shadows. We rose from our beds, shoved our belongings into our bags and left for home, feeling as though we survived something monumental.

The negative schoolmaster had won, for now.

Over time, Sandy and I became close friends with Jeff, attending more investigations together. The following year, after spending time learning more about our mediumistic abilities, we returned to Parsonsfield Seminary to challenge the schoolmaster and regain some of our power. Through our combined efforts, we were able to push him back out of the room and remove some of the confidence he gained from scaring us the first time. Barbara Williams continues to work on crossing over the wayward souls and diffuse the negative energy.

Parsonsfield Seminary still remains as one of the most haunted locations I've ever visited. I only hope in time that I can unravel more of the mysteries associated with the location. Until then, I'm just thankful for the experience.

It was when I learned that all is not what it seems.

Sometimes the history books have gaping holes.

And sometimes fear can be your best ally if you listen to it.

Joni Mayhan is a paranormal investigator and author of 12 books. She teaches Paranormal 101 classes in the town of Gardner, Massachusetts, as well as hosting on-line courses. To learn more about Joni, check out her website: Jonimayhan.com. Joni Mayhan author page on Amazon

The Ghost of Love

By Debra Robinson

I know now that love never dies. Sounds cliché, but it is a fact. This is a true story of life after death, of dealing with someone you love too much to be afraid of, even when they've returned from the afterlife.

I'm a lifelong professional musician and songwriter. The commercial recording studio we have operated in our basement for many years is of a workable size, and only a bit tight when recording bands with five or more members. On this particular night, four musicians were playing, taking turns fixing a few bad parts individually, while the others watched. My husband is the recording engineer, always at the helm on one end of the long room.

Two of the four young men sat down; one in a corner chair facing the others, and another behind the drum set. They all watched as Billy the bass player rerecorded a part he had made a mistake on earlier. Billy sat his beer behind him, on top of the dryer that shares space with the studio. Suddenly a band member in the corner chair yelled as the bottle rose in the air and smashed down on the floor in front of the bass drum. Beer splattered them all, and everyone stood with their mouths gaping open in disbelief. They had all seen the beer picked up and tossed.

But my husband realized something immediately. Billy had been a childhood friend of our son James—they had both gone into music. "Billy, the last time you were here, you recorded with James, right?"

Billy nodded solemnly, and then his face suddenly lit up with understanding. "James, you scared me, man," Billy said aloud.

"I think he's just letting you know he's still here."

James had been killed by a drunk driver several years before. This was not the first time he had made his presence known since his death. With his outrageous sense of humor and giving spirit, James had made friends far and wide, all over the world in fact. Billy knew this was the sort of demonstration James would use to get his attention. It was Billy's first trip back to the house since James's death.

James was only twenty-four when he was killed, on top of the world and in love with life. I think this may be why it was so hard for him to leave, at first, why he sometimes still comes back to check in. I want to tell nonbelievers some of the other incredible things he has showed us. If we hadn't already believed in the other side, James would have changed that by now.

In my own life, when you grow up with psychic abilities in your family, it becomes almost commonplace to have an awareness of paranormal situations in the world around you. Even though I was used to my grandmother having prophetic dreams and doling out clairvoyant tidbits to us at random times, somehow I accepted this as normal. I used my own gifts to sense things others didn't; mostly warning of danger when I was given those types of messages. Even though psychic awareness was always around me, I developed a healthy respect for these things, based on the content of my own messages and those of my grandmother. I kept my distance from it all too after some bad experiences. I came to believe in good and evil, and that we are stuck here in the middle of a constant battle between the two, a battle in which our choices matter.

Early on, I did follow a somewhat paranormal lifestyle, working for the biggest psychic hotline and doing private readings for clients. I also juggled a separate career, while I raised my only child, my son James. I had struggled to become a mother, and I adored the role. He and I grew close, and I came to realize that this love between us was bigger than any I had ever known. I loved him more than anything, even myself. I have now learned this kind of love transcends death.

As James grew up, he began proving he carried the psychic gift that ran in my mother's side of the family. As early as three years old, he was picking up my thoughts and often would speak a phrase or sentence out loud that I had just been running through my mind. It was uncanny. He came to me complaining he knew what people were going to say before they said it, and I had to school him on how to keep quiet about that, as my own mother had taught me. Over the years as he grew into young adulthood the bond between us grew unbreakable, and his own psychic abilities formidable.

He had always told us he would die young; I would distract him from this, telling him we all feel that way when we're kids. But James insisted. And then he began to have specific dreams about it as he grew older, nightmares sometimes. But he would never say exactly what he saw. He would tell his friends various crazy-sounding scenarios. James told one buddy that he, James, would have a big funeral and all his friends would come and that this particular friend would meet a redhead there and take her home with him afterward. This friend later told my husband this was exactly what happened the night of James's funeral.

James was a musician and a talented songwriter. He usually penned happy songs, but not long before the end of his life, they suddenly began to go dark. "As close to tortured as I've ever been, is lying here wondering if my heart might beat away and away and away," is an example of the lyrics that were far darker than his usual. One night I stopped at his apartment and saw he had been dabbling in oils. A huge four-foot by four-foot painting of a bloody heart leaned against one wall, realistic severed veins and arteries accurately displayed. I freaked out. "What is the deal with you and hearts lately, James?" He just shrugged and laughed. It wasn't until a few months later when I met the man who now carries James's heart inside his chest, that I understood the connection. Somehow James knew what was coming. He sensed it.

The evening James died, my husband and I came home from the hospital, having been told it was almost over, that the swelling in his brain would kill him sometime during the night. We had been there for days, devastated and exhausted. I fell into bed in a stupor, and my husband went down into the studio where he and James had spent so many wonderful hours together. He broke down and prayed aloud, talking to James, asking him not to leave us. And suddenly, the stack of papers beside where James always sat at the console, crinkled. My husband turned quickly to look, asking "Was that you?" And the crinkling sound happened again. It was almost like a plastic water bottle crackling, a static electricity sound. He knew it was James. And that he was saying goodbye.

Surrounded by friends and family the next few days, our shock was complete. How do you get through something like this? It was the sort of thing that happened to others, not to us.

My precious boy was gone. And yet, I was afraid he was somehow stuck between both worlds because he kept showing us he was still around.

As I sat on the front porch talking with a cousin I had not seen in years, suddenly a warm hand closed around my ankle. I stared at my leg, clearly feeling the hand, but not wanting to be rude and interrupt my relative. The grip lessened then went away, followed a few moments later by yelling from behind the house. James's dad, cousin and best friend were in his garage apartment, where he had a video camera pointed at the entryway hooked up to a TV. The boys had noticed a round opaque white globe-shaped ectoplasmic type object on the TV screen, coming from the front of the house down the sidewalk. It stopped right in front of the man-door of the garage, and then moved on past, to the rear of the yard. I knew then, James had grabbed my ankle and when I didn't react, he'd continued on to his Dad, out in the garage.

Our neighbor continued to see the top of James's beanie covered head coming up the drive between our houses. Her kitchen window was too tall to show much else. As all these reports kept coming from James's friends and others, I began to write them down. I constantly walked around the house telling him to go to the light, doing whatever I could to help him if he was stuck between worlds. Finally, so many things happened, I decided to write a book about it all. This helped me channel my grief, and somehow tied together all the loose ends about my son's death, connecting all the dots.

One night as I sat with a laptop on my knees, working on the book, I kept noticing a scratching sound coming from somewhere. I ignored it, assuming it was James's old dog, possibly up against the door to the kitchen, where she often slept. The door was closed, not three feet away from where I sat on the sofa. The next time I heard it, I stopped typing and listened. The noise was definitely coming from the old oak door. I resumed typing. Knock, knock, knock, knock,

knock! Five sharp raps burst from the old door over my shoulder! I called for our dog, and heard her get up far across the kitchen, her toenails clicking over to the door. That did it; it wasn't her.

I got up then and opened the door, staring at our old grizzled Lab. "Was that you James?" I asked into the silence. I glanced down at the knob, and on the wooden panel beside it, were the initials JS scratched in the wood—my son's initials. I had never seen them before and surely would have by now if they had always been there. They weren't small either—almost two inches high. Then I remembered the scratching sound I'd been hearing. The only conclusion I could come to was my son scratched his initials then knocked on the door to draw my attention to it.

Another night I was working away on the laptop when a thump came from the ceiling just above and in front of where I sat. I glanced up to spot a small white feather floating down from the ceiling. I got up to retrieve it in disbelief. There were no feathers anywhere on the main floor, and how could a feather appear from the ceiling anyway? Then I remembered something. When my mother died four years earlier, James sat beside me on a beautiful blue-sky April day at the cemetery. We were waiting for the graveside service to begin, when we saw a small white feather float down from the sky, with not a tree or a bird in sight. I asked him if he saw that, and James said he did. He wondered if it was my Mom. Afterward, he and I picked the feather up as we left. Suddenly the white feather had more significance to me; perhaps this was James's way of reminding me—because only he would know of this shared moment between us.

Another time, after six months had passed, I missed him as badly as ever. I pulled into a local park, a place where he and I had spent many happy hours when James was little. I took my lunch and climbed on top a picnic table overlooking the park. I sat on the table and kept my feet on the seat. I spoke aloud to James, telling him I missed him. I was always wistful about his loss. I got down to walk a few feet over for a closer view of the stadium, and then returned to my seat. But when I placed my foot on the wood to climb back up, a dark object now sat there. It hadn't been there a few moments ago when I'd first stepped up. Curiously, I bent to retrieve it. A guitar pick that had a scrolled "W" on one side, like the ones James used with his Washburn guitar we'd bought him for his last birthday. I understood logically this was called an apport; an object appearing out of thin air. I knew apports were often believed to be brought or placed by a spirit. Just like the feather that floated from the ceiling. I talked to James a little bit more, thanked him for the pick, and left. Any doubts I'd had about these occurrences, and particularly connecting them to James's loss, were being systematically taken away, one by one.

Random things continue to happen, at least, things that make us suspicious of them being signs from James. Sometimes, we feel a light patting on top our heads when we sit on the couch. James used to walk past and do this sometimes. My husband and I, and two of my friends were all in the studio when several knocks sounded from the studio door. We were the only ones in the house at the time. One day, I drove out to the cemetery to see James's grave. I had been very ill, and unable to go for months. I spoke to James the whole way, even sat there talking for a few moments before I got out at the cemetery. I shut the car off, and suddenly, the dome light came on slowly, increasing to full brightness, and then fading away. The car was off so I was astonished. I asked out loud if it was James. The light again came on gradually, achieved its full brightness then faded slowly. I nearly broke down in tears. I sat at his grave a long time that day, aware of the energy it must've taken to accomplish the feats he'd achieved. Above all, I wanted him to know he is not forgotten by us and those he left behind.

I've heard whistling, long phrases of singing, and many times, the squeak of someone walking in our upstairs hallway. My husband has heard this too, as well as footsteps coming up the driveway when out in our backyard.

We've witnessed lights at the windows when our house is dark and empty, sounds of walking in our upstairs rooms when we are downstairs, a piece of paper pulled out of the printer tray right before our eyes, and once, paper stored securely in the studio dumped unceremoniously on the floor. It makes me wonder if James wants to write something, and whether he could accomplish this. At this point, with the level of phenomena that have already occurred, I believe it may only be a matter of time before he does.

Above all, what I want to say to each and every one of you reading this story is that death is not the end. No, we do not know exactly what it will look like there. I am hoping it is a wonderful place we all can go to be with our loved ones. Even if religion is wrong, and there is only a gray space where spirits mingle around, at least, we can be with those who have gone before us.

James seems much more at peace than he was in those early days after his death. For this I am grateful. I love him now as much, maybe even more, than I ever did. I long to see him again, and I believe he is still able to see and interact with us occasionally when he chooses. But I mostly want to believe he has other work to do now, that he is at peace, and simply waiting for us to join him when it's our turn.

The book I wrote about James's life, death and afterlife is titled "A Haunted Life". It has led me to a new career as an author—sometimes when one door closes, as they say, another opens. Lastly, I want to tell you all to stay in the light, believe in your gut instincts, listen to your dreams, and love as deeply as you can, because truly, love lasts forever.

Debra Robinson is the author of 7 books including "A Haunted Life" Debra Robinson's website. Debra Robinson on Amazon.

DEVIL'S MOON

By William Lester, Ph. D.

FIELD JOURNAL
Assoc. Prof. WM. Lester
Abizanda (Spain)
Sept. 29, 1992

We drove a few miles and parked at the crest of a bluff overlooking a series of mostly barren fields. There was little greenery, save the occasional patch of scrub. The sun had already sunk beneath the rim of the world. My companion, Sergio, revealed from a case a 6.5x54 caliber Mannlicher-Schoenauer. Looking out across the landscape, he said to me: "Ahora vamas a esperar." (Now we will wait)...

We waited there on the bluff for what seemed like hours, but I realized later that no more than 20 minutes had expired before the most horrific sound I had ever heard came rushing across the landscape. It was not exactly a howl-- nor was it a scream. It was, upon reflection, a preternatural wail heralding the fulfillment of a curse.

Sergio advised me to take my field glass and look to the left at about 75 yards. My field of vision was illuminated by an impossibly bright, full moon. So was the view through the scope of Sergio's rifle.

As the baneful wail began to echo down to nothing, I saw it. I saw it running at a tremendous speed. I could even make out the dust kicked up by clawed feet ripping across the ground. Although clearly inhuman, I could detect the vestiges of clothing-- ripped, torn, and flailing in the air stirred by the motion of the thing. It took large loping strides and strangely, its arms barely moved-- as if they were unnecessary for generating torque.

It was at just that moment of my contemplation, that Sergio fired a shot...

The shot shook me to my core. Yet, I saw the bullet strike and take the thing to the ground. Then, to my horror, it rose again, in what were mere moments. I watched as it quickly resumed its surreal, digitigrade loping across the dark landscape. I couldn't believe what I was seeing. That shot, through the midsection, would have killed any man ever born, and yet this monstrosity was knocked down by nothing more than the force of the bullet. Then Sergio fired again.

The second shot struck the thing in the upper arm or shoulder, for I saw the ragged shirt flare upon impact and a patch of it blew off. The beast did not fall this time, but was pushed by the strike-- only momentarily, before if continued its mad sprint. Sergio got off one more round before the thing finally dashed out of our field of vision. Again, that terrible wail exploded in the darkness all around us.

I realized that we were now vulnerable to an attack-- from virtually any direction. Would the wolf-man seek escape, or, as I feared, seek to exact vengeance upon us? Certainly if Sergio's rifle had failed to stop the beast, there was little hope of success in a hand to hand confrontation. In any other situation, we would have been more than a match for an assailant. I was 24 years old at the time. Although Sergio was ten years my senior, we were both well over six feet tall and easily capable of giving a good account of ourselves.

We agreed, however, with a glance and a nod, that indeed discretion was the better part of valor. As we headed back to the jeep, I found myself muttering and musing aloud-- what in God's name was that? And Sergio replied, in a rare smattering of English-- "Nothing in God's name. That was the hombre lobo."

We came to learn that the monstrous fiend that haunted the hills, woods, and quiet roads amongst the villages, was a WOLF-MAN (El Hombre Lobo)-- a thing quite different from the so-called werewolf of legend. It was a man-- cursed-- possessed, as it were, by a bestial, dark spirit that waged war with the soul of the man it sought to subdue and imprison. As such, the demon was brought to the fore when the forces of evil were at their strongest-- especially in conjunction with the coming of the full moon. Unlike the natural wolf, the murderous abomination walked on two legs, at times even adorned in the shredded remnants of the man's clothing. Strangely, until the time of the Blood Moon, the eyes retained a saddened human quality

We learned from the villagers that the burning of sulfur was prone to keeping away wolves. The scent permeated the air in the village square and the adjoining pathways. One night, we ventured out-- against strenuous admonitions, to investigate the strange happenings. This was the night that I was to experience the preternatural reality of the horror that has haunted me, lo, these many years. What I witnessed that night has never left me and the nightmarish visage is a constant companion. It reminds me that at times, that the devil does indeed walk the Earth.

Excerpt From the Journal of Sergio Morales...(AS translated by Associate Prof. WM. Lester)
****
"Last night the thing appeared in the field below the village. The professor too witnessed the creature. I am sure now that he is convinced, as I have been, for some time, that this was an unnatural thing. Three times, my rifle found its target and yet the howling devil endures. I spoke today with Senor Abizanda and Sgt. Gomez. They have agreed to consult with the professor. Is it possible that together we can rid this village of its terrible curse?"

The body of night watchman Jose Mancia was found inside his small two-room office building on the morning of October 1st. He had been beaten and pummeled with unimaginable force. His face and throat had been ripped and torn as if by the claws of a raving beast. Abizanda was a small hamlet and word of the horror spread like the plague.

Item....The previously installed security camera revealed a brief moment of the deed, but little more. The tape itself was viewed by local officials before being secreted away.

Item....The killer was possessed of incredible strength. The metal door, locked and bolted from the inside, had been forcefully pulled from the hinges and slung thirty feet.

Item...The momentary flash of activity revealed by the tape indicated that the killer was in fact, the same impossible monstrosity recently witnessed by Sergio and myself dashing across the fields below the town.

This is as much as I dare reveal to you here. Suffice it to say, that such horror exists in this world. Though I wish it was not so, failure to disclose the reality of such things would for me, be the highest form of hypocrisy. I have seen it. I have witnessed it and it has been like a plague of nightmares upon me since those long ago days.

So, what do you think? There may perhaps be as many reactions to this experience as eyes that read it. I am, therefore, quite content to leave the burden of final judgment to you.

If what you read horrifies or shocks you—and has forever changed your concept of reality, allow me to offer you one small glint of relief. Tell yourself, as I have, day after day, night after night, that it's only a story. If you can do that much, you can convince yourself that behind the safety of your door, in the quiet of your bed, that it couldn't happen here.

Dr. William Lester is the Director of the Institute of Metaphysics and the host of Shadowland Radio Show

INTO THE VEIL AND BACK

By Alan Wright

Through the years, I have had many experiences of the paranormal kind. I'm a healer and an empath. I'm also a passive medium. I have dreams. I don't have any control over them. That being said I would like to write about the ones that have left the biggest impression on me.

After my Grandfather died in 1982 I was in a bad way because I missed him and I wasn't really sure where he was in the afterlife. I was raised that if you believed in God you would go to heaven but you could also go to hell.

After I had come home from work one day I got ready for bed that evening. Sometime during the night, I had a dream, one which I will remember for the rest of my life.

I remember waking and seeing this body on this gurney. I was watching this scene from above the body in the corner of the ceiling of the room. It was at this time that I looked and realized that it was my body lying on that gurney. There was a doctor and a nurse working on my body like they were trying to revive me.

It was at this time that I started moving. I was moving up through the ceiling of the room. I kept moving upward through the roof of the building. I kept moving upward and I was moving faster and faster.

As I was moving upward I was looking down on the Earth. I thought what a beautiful planet that we live on. I then thought how such a beautiful planet could have so much sorrow and sadness with the wars, killings, and rapes. Every kind of bad thing that could happen to a person happens on this planet. I'm not even talking about the things that humans are doing to the Earth itself.

I then heard a voice. This voice came to me like someone talking to me in my mind but there was nobody there with me. This voice said, "the Earth is fulfilling the purpose for which it was created." The next thing I thought about was my sins and the things I had done in my life that might not be considered ethical. The Voice came to me again and it said that "I was where I was supposed to be at that time."

It said, because of the choices I had made in my life, they had made me stronger and that those choices had made me where I was at this point. I then thought about my family and how they were going to make it without me. The Voice came to me again and said: "the hardships that I went through in my life they would have to go through also so that they too could be strong and be at the place that I was at."

It was at this time that I realized that I was picking up more speed and the Earth beneath me was quickly disappearing and that I was among the stars. The stars are different colors. I never saw colors of the stars on earth.

I was moving faster and faster and it started getting darker and darker and then I got the feeling that I was in a tunnel like people that had near death experiences said that they went through but I didn't feel like I was inside of a structure but it did feel like a tunnel.

The next thing that caught my attention was a light at the end of the tunnel. It was small at first but bigger and brighter the closer I got to it.

As I got closer to the light I realized that there was a being inside this light and that the light was coming from this being. I was getting closer to the light and then I went into the light. It was one of the most beautiful things that ever happened to me.

The Light was love. This light that was coming from this person was love. This love was not like the love that we talk about this love was a thing.

It had substance and you could feel it. It went right through me like a knife. It touched every part of my body. It was a searching love that if I had any guilt in me it would have found it.

As I got closer to this person I passed out.

When I woke up I was in a type of meadow with tall grass. As I was laying there I could hear the birds and I heard the water in a creek nearby. As I stood there, I noticed that there was a group of people who had surrounded me. I felt like I knew everyone in that circle. They were friends and family members that had passed on before me.

The person who had my attention was the one that was standing right in front of me. It was my Grandfather. He started talking to me but he did not move his lips. He was talking to me he was talking to my mind. I felt like I could speak if I wanted to but I didn't have to. He expressed his love to me and me to him.

We then started walking on this path that surrounded this Meadow. The people there were wearing white robes. They were a brilliant white. The colors in this place were brilliant. The greens, the flowers were so beautiful that it is hard to describe.

The last thing I remember is walking with my Grandfather side by side on this path. He was telling me something but I don't remember what it was. I feel since I'm older now that he was telling me to hold the course and that I could be reunited with him later.

This experience changed my life. I knew now that there is a place we go when we die. My Grandfather was all right.

****

Now I 'm going to tell you about the other time I had to go through the veil again. This time was just about a month ago.

Again I went to bed and feel asleep. I had this dream where I went through the veil. This time, it was very different. There was no tunnel or a bright light.

There was nothing but darkness; there were no colors just shadows. I could see buildings off in the distance but the people did not stay in them. The people in this place stayed in the shadows. The people there were in disparate circumstances. It seemed that they had committed things that they were ashamed of. These people stayed in the shadows because of the crimes they had done.

I tried to talk to one person that I felt was the reason I was there but he would not step out of the darkness where I could see him or talk to him. He kept saying something about killing someone and that person he killed was there also and that was the reason why he didn't want to step out of the shadows. He felt that the person he killed in real life would find him.

When I woke up I could not get over the feeling of dread and depression that I had from being in this place. I felt sad for these people who were there.

I feel through my experiences that I have been to a place called heaven and a place called hell. But I think that these two places are staging areas and that they are not the final resting places for these people. I feel that my experiences have given me a different perspective of things. I believe that there are places for the good and places for the disobedient. I believe in a God and I believe in a life after death. I believe that I have been to those places.

Alan Wright is the author of "Through the Veil and Back; Chronicles of a Healer and Passive Medium" and "At the Edge of Infinity" (March 2016) Alan Wright's Author Page on Amazon

Fifty Minutes of Missing Time

By Rod C. Davis

Shortly after my wife and I met during the summer of 1960, we had our first supernatural experience together, and they have continued ever since. Some years have been far more active than others, i.e. 1979, beginning June 1st, and ending on August 25th. During that time, we lived in a house that harbored very unfriendly spirits, and all family members, including our pets, experienced traumatic events, some of which left mental scars for years to come.

Over time, I developed an overwhelming desire to understand the unexplainable experiences that we had been encountering, and during the early '70s, I began to research the supernatural and paranormal. I've interviewed numerous people that have had sporadic experiences similar to ours over the years, but nothing in their history, or ours, compares to the barrage of events that have been transpiring since 2003. On April 26, 2003, and on April 26, 2004, something happened to convince me that each encounter has a message embedded in it, and following is an accounting of events from my journal that support that assumption.

It is my firm belief that these supernatural and paranormal encounters that I am sharing with you began as a result of a trip my wife and I made to Pagosa Springs, Colorado on March 26th, 2003. The first evening in Pagosa Springs opened up a whole new world to us.

While eating dinner in one of the local restaurants, my wife and I talked about the business meeting we had earlier in the day, and somewhere in that conversation an idea flashed into my mind, which was nothing more than an impulse to tell our waitress that I was an author that writes about the supernatural and paranormal. When I asked her if she knew of anyone in town that has had any of those type experiences, I got much more than I expected.

We ended up talking with several people in the restaurant who shared with us some very interesting paranormal events they experienced, and most of them had happened within the past twelve months. In addition to all of the information we gathered, I was given the phone numbers to people who had supernatural encounters. Two and a half hours later my wife and I left the restaurant with referrals to several people, both in and out of town, and both of us were tingling with excitement.

During the next two days, I was given additional referrals and ended up interviewing seven people in all. Many of the experiences that were shared with me had distinct similarities. Several of the women that I interviewed told me they believed the flying objects and entities that they had seen were associated with Archuleta Mesa, and each of them took the time to share with me some of that area's history. Shortly after our return to Las Vegas, Nevada I spent a solid two weeks on the Internet, from early morning until late evening, researching any and all information that I could find on Dulce, New Mexico, Archuleta Mesa, Sandia, and Los Alamos. None of the information was recent, but it was my first exposure to it.

While conducting my Internet research I printed out the information that was not an obvious hoax, and I spent many hours pouring over that material. I had a great deal of difficulty coming to grips with certain aspects of the data I read, and before going to sleep the night of April 25th, I decided to give Wesley Bateman a call the next morning. In addition to being an author and accomplished physicist, he is also telepathic. It was Mr. Bateman's telepathic abilities that gave Gene Roddenberry numerous ideas for his productions, and I have been fortunate enough to spend many mesmerizing and educational hours with him.

99

It is important to note that Wesley had been receiving telepathic communications over a long period of time from beings in another universe, and it was those communications, along with 25 years of research in the field of Sacred Geometry, that helped him to rediscover the Ra system of Mathematics.

On April 26th, as I was driving east on Desert Inn Road, on my way to a meeting at the Rio Casino, I called Wes Bateman, and his daughter answered. Wes had worked too late in the night and was still asleep, so she told me to call back in about two hours. At that point, I was at a stoplight on Rainbow Boulevard and Desert Inn. The light turned green just as I ended the call, and I checked the dash clock in the van to see what time I should call back. I noted that it was 10:30 AM (at least I thought it was).

Just after crossing over Rainbow, I felt a shimmering type sensation pass through the upper half of my body, front to back. I shook my head trying to understand what the heck that was all about when I saw a street sign coming up. I was in total confusion when it turned out to be Arville Street, especially since the next intersection after Rainbow was Torrey Pines.

Arville was past the point where I had intended to turn off Desert Inn and cross over to Flamingo

Road, and my confusion grew to new heights when I saw that the clock on my dash still read 10:30 AM. Arville is a little over 2.5 miles from Rainbow, and light Saturday morning traffic or not, it is not possible to travel 2.5 miles through Las Vegas in less than a minute. As luck would have it, Arville was an OK place to be since the next major intersection was Desert Inn and Valley View Boulevard, and the Rio Casino just happens to be on the corner of Valley View and Flamingo. But then again, was it really luck, or was it providence?

One of the individuals that I was meeting at the Rio was an accomplished dowser, and based on what I have seen him do, I have a deep respect for his skills. I explained to him what had just happened to me, and after asking me a couple of questions he nonchalantly said that I had passed through a portal. A longtime friend of his sitting at the table agreed with him, and that explanation temporarily satisfied my need for an answer. But, as hard as I tried, I could not remember anything from the time that I had crossed over Rainbow and found myself at Arville, and my mind kept working on that void.

When I spoke with Wes Bateman later that day and queried him regarding the research that I had done on the Internet, I also told him about what happened to me after I talked with his daughter that morning. I was somewhat disappointed when he did not have much to say about the incident, and during a conversation about 6 weeks later he finally said to me, "I think that you were pulled aside and given some information for future use."

On April 28, 2003, my wife and I left for the New England states to attend numerous book signings, and I shared my experience with many of the people that I met. A few of them had asked me if I lost anytime during the event, and I reminded them that when I crossed over Rainbow it was 10:30 AM, and it was still 10:30 AM when I found myself at Arville. So, no time lost, right?

But something started to gnaw at the back of my mind after I talked with the woman who had lost almost two hours of time, and shortly after that meeting, something weird began to happen. Whenever I looked at the dash clock in my van, 9:30 AM flashed before my eyes, and it was actually sometime in the afternoon. After it happened four or five times I told my wife what I had been seeing, and also told her that perhaps it was 9:30 when I called my friend, and not 10:30.

On May 11th, while in Carrabassett Valley, Maine we met a Spiritual Medium named Mary Robbins, and she told me that I was going to meet three people that would be very influential in my life. She said that one of them was a woman located in Pennsylvania, Ohio or New York and that the second one was in the Midwest (but she could not get specific as to which state), and that the third was in the Black Hills. She did not know where the Black Hills were, but she was able to elaborate on numerous circumstances and nuances surrounding the last individual.

Shortly after we returned to Las Vegas, I asked my wife to get my cellular phone bill for the month of April, and my suspicion was confirmed. When I saw the exact time that I had called my friend a chill ran through my body. According to the itemized bill, the call was made at 9:40 AM. I had lost 50 minutes of time, and I wish I knew, or could remember what was going on during that event. Then again, maybe I don't want to know.

There is more to this incident. During the book-signing trip, on more than one occasion my wife saw someone standing over her when she woke up during the night, and when she went to wake me, they disappeared. To our knowledge, there was not any loss of time during those occurrences. Something else did happen though that was not part of our norm. Whenever getting back to Vegas from a long trip, it usually takes me a couple of days to get my old zip back. But that wasn't the case this time.

We had been back for a week, and each morning when I got up I was very tired. When I woke up on the eighth morning, I was not only dead tired, my body ached like I was coming down with the flu. Fortunately, the only symptom that I experienced was the aching, and that was gone sometime before noon. As I was standing at the kitchen sink filling the coffee pot that morning I looked out into the backyard, and I was mystified when I saw that our lawn was carpeted with a circle of white oleander flowers. The circle was 15 feet in diameter, and right below our bedroom window. The oleander flowers never end up on our lawn, even when we get a good windstorm. They always end up in the desert landscape that surrounds the bushes.

There's another event that I believe was connected with this incident. For the next 10 days after I saw that circle of oleander flowers on our lawn, I got a metallic taste in my mouth every time I discussed anything about my loss of time, Dulce, or Archuleta Mesa.

Lots of thoughts have gone through my mind since I discovered that loss of time, and I keep mentally rehashing the event, over and over again. I did most of my research regarding Dulce and Archuleta Mesa on the Internet. We all know that the Internet is an open media that can be easily monitored. I just wonder if my loss of time on April 26th, and the metallic type of taste in my mouth, had anything to do with the considerable amount of time that I spent on the Internet researching Dulce and Archuleta Mesa.

A couple weeks after my wife and I returned to Las Vegas from the book-signing trip, I met with Edward Schultz, a Cherokee Indian, who is a past president of the Las Vegas Desert Dowsers. I told him about the person that I was supposed to meet in the Black Hills, and I asked him if he could dowse where the Black Hills might be. He dowsed several state maps before he told me that the Black Hills in question were in Southeastern Arizona, and after a while he said that it was a woman that I was looking for and that she was not a North American Indian. He also said that she goes up on very high mesas in the Black Hills to meditate. This information later became very integral to the paranormal pattern that had been developing.

About two weeks after I met with Mr. Schultz, a friend of his that is a psychic and dowser came into town. She has done work for the FBI and police departments to locate missing people and items. Ed introduced me to her because he thought that she would be able to give me a better insight on the woman that I was searching for, and she did. She told me that the woman I was looking for is a North American Indian, that she had had significant health problems, and to not waste my time looking for her because she was always on the move. As it turned out, what she told me, coupled with the information provided by Mary Robbins, helped to identify the woman in a chance meeting almost a year later.

* * *

Another series of paranormal events began on August 2, 2003, one of which is still occurring as of the date of this writing, January 26, 2016. An accounting of those events, which is titled, 'A Few Days of the Paranormal,' can be viewed on www.rodcdavis.com, under UFO, Paranormal, and Spiritual Experiences. One of the events, which happened on August 14th, eventually ties four people together, Wesley Bateman, Debra Moore, Monarca Merrifield and me. And, a meeting between Debra Moore, Wes Bateman and I, which I will soon reveal, brought to light the reason behind my 50 minutes of missing time.

On August 14th, an invisible entity made itself known to me, and an hour later I was poked at the base of my rib cage, to the right of the sternum, 2 hours later. The force of the jab woke and knocked the wind out of me, and the noise I made woke my wife. The invisible entity that came that night is still with me. However, I have not been poked real hard just below my rib cage, as I had been the first time, although there have been many occasions that I have been poked hard enough in the same spot, to make me grunt. On several occasions, I was fully awake when I felt the jabs.

The morning of August 15th, I called Wes Bateman to tell him about the events that I had been experiencing since August 2nd, and he seemed to be very interested. I told him that I had to be in Arizona within a couple of days and that I'd like to stop by his home for a visit. While there I pointed to the spot where I had been poked, and he told me that was the exact same location where he has had an almost constant pain for a long time. He said that his doctors had put him through extensive tests, but after exhausting all possibilities, they were unable to find the cause. During that visit, Wes told me that he believes the beings that have been telepathically communicating with him over the years, have been the instigators of my experiences. He felt that they were making these events happen so that I would tell him about them, but he was not 100% sure why.

While doing some additional research on Archuleta Mesa during June 2003, I met the woman in the East that Mary Robbins had told me about. She was living in Pennsylvania, grew up in New York, and was looking for a home in Ohio.

She has been very influential in my life since, and she has had extensive personal UFO experiences.

On April 16th, 2004, I met Debra Moore, a Cherokee Indian, at a business meeting. As we talked I steadily developed a feeling about her that I could not identify, and on an impulse I reached across the table and held my hand out palm side up. I told Debra to place her hand over mine about an inch away. The force that I felt was very intense, and she felt it also. Both of us immediately got goose bumps all over our body.

As we talked I learned that she was from Arizona and that because she's always on the move she uses an address in Dolan Springs as her permanent mailing address. When she told me where she was from, I asked her if she ever went to the Black Hills, and she said, "Yes. I go up on the highest mesas to meditate." Later in the conversation, she told me that she had been very sick and that she had been placed in a hospice to die.

Debra wasn't ready to die and willed herself to get better. Today you'd never know that she had been on the brink of death or a paraplegic. I was very impressed with this woman and was beginning to firmly believe that she was the person in the Black Hills that Mary Robbins had told me about. Later in that conversation, Debra made a statement that convinced me that she was THE woman. She told me that she had a pain at the base of her rib cage, and when she pointed to the location, it was in the exact same spot as Mr. Bateman's, and the same place in which I had been poked. She said at one point the doctors thought that the pain might have been caused by her gallbladder, so they removed it, but the pain did not go away. She has had extensive tests, the same ones as Wes, yet they could not find the cause of the pain.

During the next week I met with Debra several more times, and each of the circumstances and nuances that Mary Robbins had shared with me regarding the person in the Black Hills, all came to pass. I developed a very strong feeling that Debra, Wes, and I should have a joint meeting to see if there was some kind of a synergy between us, and I called Mr. Bateman to get his opinion. He agreed that we should meet, and also said that a visit would be in order since he had a package he wanted me to deliver to someone in Las Vegas. I checked with Debra to see if she would be interested in taking a trip to Arizona to meet Wes, and she agreed.

On April 26, 2004, Debra's next day off, she and I went to meet with Wes. I do not know what I expected to happen when we were all together in one room, but no bells, whistles or sirens went off. The conversation bounced from one topic to another, and eventually the subject became space travel. When Wes was in the middle of explaining how space ships travel over great distances in a short period of time, his eyes and mine locked. As soon as they did I felt a vibrating sensation that blanketed my entire forehead, and it felt like it encompassed the entire front section of my brain. It was the same type of a vibrating sensation that I felt one year earlier, on April 26, 2003, just as I crossed over Rainbow Blvd. on Desert Inn Road. But then again it was different. It did not pass through the whole upper half of my body as it did a year earlier. It was focused and stayed in one location the whole time.

The moment I felt that sensation, Wes stopped talking in mid-sentence. I saw the space between him and me change instantly, and it was like I was looking at him through thick glass or very clear water. Then I saw a thin line that was about three-eighths to a half inch thick, and the width of Wesley's head, travel from me to him, and it kind of shimmered like heat rising off of a tar road during the summer. The event that transpired between Wes and me lasted 2 to 3 seconds, but Mr. Bateman was quiet for about 10 to 15, and then continued.

Once he finished, I asked him why he had stopped talking a few minutes ago. His face developed a blank look, and it appeared that he did not realize what he had done. Debra confirmed that he had stopped talking, and when I told him what I saw happen between him and me, he said, "That was The Outer State communicating to you through me."

Before Debra and I left he handed me the package that he wanted to be delivered to a person in Space Sciences, Inc. in Las Vegas. He told me what the package contained, and said that it was the smoking gun that they were looking for. He also said that he had prepared that package a while ago, but did not mail it because something told him to wait, and when I called to suggest a visit, he assumed I was the reason.

On the morning of April 27th, I called the individual at Space Sciences, Inc. and asked for an audience. We met at 11:30 that morning and ended up spending about 30 minutes together. I gave him background on both Mr. Bateman and me. When we parted company, he said that he didn't think he'd be able to get to the information until next week. My senses told me something different, and as it turned out, I was right. He called Wes early the next morning and they had a meaningful conversation.

Mr. Bateman called me after speaking with the individual from Space Sciences, Inc., and said that they had talked for about thirty minutes. During that conversation, he also told me that he had made a major breakthrough in his work on the first SETI message that morning. My mind instantly flashed back to my 50 minutes of missing time, and to May of 2003, when Wes told me that I had been pulled aside and given some information for future use. I found it interesting that just the afternoon before I had seen the thin shimmering line pass from me to Wes. Perhaps I had been given information for future use.

It is my opinion that the meeting with the individual at Space Sciences, Inc., and his follow up phone call to Wes the next day, could be the beginning of many good things to come for the benefit of mankind and that there is a story in all of this that should be told. Someday I hope to be the author or co-author that tells it.

In conclusion, on April 27th, 2004, I had a conversation with Monarca Merrifield. I asked her if she recalled that I had been poked by something about seven to eight inches to the right of my sternum, just below my rib cage while lying in bed. When she said, "Yes," I told her about Debra and Wes, each having a pain in that same location, and that I was certain it bonded us together for some common purpose. That is when I learned that she too had a pain in the same location for years and that she has had the same tests as Wes and Debra, but as with them, the cause is still unknown.

Mary Robbins told me I would meet three people who would be very influential in my life. I find it very interesting that two of them have a common denominator, a pain to the right of their sternum, just below their rib cage. By the way, Wesley Bateman turned out to be the third person Mary Robbins described to me.

Reverend Rod C. Davis website rodcdavis.com
Rod is the author of The Miracle of Three Physical Signs from God, Direct Contact by God Volume 1 *and* Direct Contact by God Volume 2

Sackets Harbor Battlefield NY

By Dennis Gager

Sackets Harbor is a village located in Jefferson County New York at Lake Ontario. It was founded in 1801 by Augustus Sackett, a land speculator from New York City. This was a very significant location during the War of 1812. The Navy built shipyards and made it the Great Lakes Navy Headquarters. The Army had forts and barracks to house 3,000 soldiers stationed there to protect the shipyard. Two battles were fought here during the war of 1812.

In August 2011, I was a part of a paranormal investigation team. I was out on my first investigation as a member. My team Leader told us that we were invited by an employee at Sackets Harbor, NY to come up and do an investigation of the old battlefield grounds where many significant battles had taken place from the French and Indian War to countless others. The Employee claimed that he personally has heard musket shots going off and heard his name being called repeatedly until he was actually being shoved. He said many of the staff there has had similar experiences as well.

Our team leader set up a investigation there. We arrived early and took statements from the staff.

This is such a beautiful area, surrounded by the lake. I stood there in awe of the scenery but also somber knowing what happened here with so many casualties and lost lives. Does the past echo in the present with the souls of the men who perished?

The moment we stepped out onto the battlefield the energy felt different. It's hard to describe what it's like. I got a feeling of sadness and heaviness. Strange smells fill the air. I noticed that my cell phone battery started to drain quickly. I went back to my vehicle to grab a spare, and it went back to being fully charged somehow when I was no longer on the field. I made a note of that on my recorder. After I finished taking notes, I went to double check the file on my audio to make sure I got everything correctly. I was amazed to hear marching and talking in the background with my voice notes and no one was around me. I immediately told the team leader and he documented it and we went and set up the equipment around the field.

We set up motion cameras in various locations on the trails where movement has been claimed to be seen. We set up audio recorders at the canyons there. Then we waited for nightfall.

As it grew darker I was a mixture of curiosity, eagerness and yet also slightly apprehensive as this was the first investigation I had been at and some amazing things had already happened. It was thought that the paranormal activity would increase in the night. This place was so awe inspiring that it was almost intimidating. Being surrounded by the blackness of night was the most intriguing thing in the world and yet it came with a quickening heartbeat sense of anxiety.

Our team leader and I took the first lap around the grounds while the other members sat at base camp. We walked around and conducted EVP sessions with no luck this time. Finally, I suggested that I go over by the cannons and try recording some audio there by myself. We were still able to see each other, but we spread out to cover more ground. So we did that. What I didn't know was that the team leader asked the spirits to do something to me to prove to him they were really there. And at the moment, he did that I felt a rush of hot air come at me and it felt like I hit a solid wall. I was caught off guard but I recovered quickly and checked the air temperature around me it was up to 72 but the temperature in that area was previously 60. I recovered from that stunning moment and I went over and told my leader what happened. He was amazed and told me what he asked the spirits to do. Needless to say, I wasn't too happy about being used as a guinea pig, but I let it go.

We went on and continued the investigation until the early morning hours then called it a night packed our equipment. The next day we sat down and went over audio and cameras. The moment I experienced the hot air right before I got shoved you could hear footsteps coming toward me. And better yet by the cannon the motion camera caught an image of a man standing there glowing white hot on camera! Things were happening around me that I could not see or hear and the evidence was shocking.

When we switched places with the other members later we went back to base command and the other group went out to the field. We monitored the DVR system and watched the team conduct their investigation. I noticed an orb form next to one of the team members by the cannon where they were now at. They jumped when they saw the orb. It rose up into the air and took off. The investigators gave chase and it disappeared into a stone.

Later on, after about an hour went by I kept getting a feeling like we were being watched. We turned around and we saw a shadow move to the right of us and vanish behind a tree. We saw this happen over and over again at different times.

At the end of the investigation our team leader went to radio the team to wrap it up but before he could use radio a high pitched screeching came over the radio and what sounded like a voice in the background. We couldn't make out what it said but there was definitely something there. This was emotional for us as it seemed like a shrill cry of pain or despair.

One of the team member's cameras turned on by itself and a high pitch sound came through it too. She swore she saw someone run by her there but it was so quick she said no one possibly could move that fast.

We went on and continued the investigation until the early morning hours then called it a night packed our equipment. The next day we sat down and went over audio and cameras. The moment I experienced the hot air right before I got shoved you could hear footsteps coming toward me. And better yet by the cannon the motion camera caught an image of a man standing there glowing white hot on camera! Things were happening around me that I could not see or hear and the evidence was shocking.

The area is very beautiful you can stand there and watch the giant lake around it. I think to myself when I was there that this is the same view the soldiers saw during battle and how could a place so beautiful have such a violent and negative past.

Dennis Gager is an author of 5 children's books including the Billy Rabbit Adventure Series, "Billy Rabbit Saves Christmas," "Billy Rabbit's Big Race," and "Billy Rabbit's Snow Day" Dennis is the author of the bestselling Sci-fi Western, "Storm to the Past," and the brand new, "Unforseen Responses"

Dennis and his wife Tiffani-Beth are the owners of DTM Wicked Radio. www.dtmwickedradio.com Dennis Gager author page on Amazon

Rochester Apartments

By Michael T. Vara

My story takes place in 2005; I am Michael Vara, host of Late Night in the Midlands Radio Show. I agreed to help remodel a building on a side street in Rochester, N.Y. little did I know that my life and my views on the paranormal would change forever.

Two close friends of mine had purchased the site, which had been damaged due to a fire. To make things a bit more easy for me, they offered to let me live in one of the studio apartments within the building.

It was a big jump from the very small bedroom I was renting at the time and it was a chance to have my place and some independence for a change.

I moved into the apartment in November and began to set up the place right away. But there was one big problem.

It did not take long to figure out that something was not right there. That very first night, it all began and folks, keep in mind that this place had been out of commission for several years because of the bad fire.

Tired from moving, my stepson and I decided to kick back and watch Smallville. We had the complete series and it involved no lifting! That night as we relaxed and watched the show, I began to hear what sounded like the kitchen cabinets opening just enough to bounce back and make that tap, tap, tap sound I would pause the show and listen.

My stepson and I both heard the sounds. Finally, I got up to turn on the kitchen light fast and (saw) nothing. This went on several times that night. My stepson and I spent some time talking and decided to call it a night.

At 3:20 AM, out of nowhere, my stereo came on blasting loudly. It nearly scared the both of us out of our skin, as we laughed and then joked that the place might be haunted.

Thinking no more of it, we both went back to bed.

The next morning my stepson told me that he kept hearing noise in the kitchen all night. And the same thing happened the following night with both the cabinets tapping and the stereo coming on right at 3:20 a.m.

By my third night, I decided I would do some research on the computer to see if I could find anything on this building.

However, as soon as I tried to do so, my computer died.

I turned it off and then a few minutes later on again, and again it would lose power.

After this happened several more times and only when searching for information on the building, I had had enough.

I was surprised because it was a brand new desktop computer and still covered by the store so I brought it in to the kind Asian man who owned the store. I left it with him for the day and said I would pick it up later.

When he went back to the store, the man said, nothing was wrong and he ran it all day. I would end up bringing the computer back to the store three more times until finally he yelled at me figuring I was pulling a fast one on him.

He said, "Nothing is wrong with the computer! I ran it all day! Are you trying to pull a fast one now? Do not come back in again!"

By that time, I was thinking, oh boy! What is going on here? I also began to wonder if mice were the culprits. Always a rational man I figured that would explain the kitchen cabinet doors opening and the critters might have chewed through the wires in the walls as well. To deal with the problem, I called an exterminator first.

While he found no evidence of mice, he set traps and planned to check back in a few days.

We never did catch anything in those traps. I also called two different electricians to check the wires and make sure everything was safe. Both electricians said the same thing, "Nothing is wrong with your wiring at all."

By then my stepson and I had contended with the constant noise, the stereo blasting in the night and the loss of power to my computer anytime I tried to find the history of this apartment building for a couple of weeks. Now if that weren't annoying enough, things started to pick up and I do mean pick up!

One night while my stepson and I were relaxing, we witnessed the blinds on the windows begin to start lifting away from the wall and then slap back at the wall. This went on for about five minutes; I should add that the apartment had radiators with no fan-blown heat.

When the blinds stopped, I went to the store and bought the movie White Noise because I wanted to see the extras at the end where they showed how to do an EVP (electronic voice phenomenon) session. I got an old tape recorder and bought brand new cassette tapes. We planned to do EVPs later that night.

The evening began with the arrival of a woman friend who was coming over to meet me. Things were going great but then the unexpected happened again.

Out of nowhere, a picture of my kids came off the wall and dropped in between us. I then started to explain to her that we suspected the place was haunted.

Later that night, I walked the woman to her car and headed back inside the building.

I opened my door and began walking in the apartment when a horseshoe that was screwed into the wall came off and just missed my head! Make no mistake about it, it could not just fall out of the wall and be thrown across the room unless someone did it. There was only my stepson and me there at that time.

Distressed by the night's events, I decided to talk on the phone to the woman who had left there hours before and just rest on my bed. Well, there's no rest for the wicked, as they say!

My stepson noticed the mouse on my computer moving by itself and then it began clicking things. My son comes in the room and said, "Dad do you see that?" Then my son added, "OMG, dad, get up and look at this!"

What I saw on the computer screen simply blew me away.

It was the newspaper story of the fire in my building several years ago and it went on to talk about two people - one child and one adult - who died in that fire. The father died trying to leave the building and the little girl died hiding in the closet in my bedroom.

I then understood another thing that had been happening each night. I always closed and secured my bedroom closet at night but in the morning, I would find it wide open. Despite how warm it was outside, this closet was always freezing cold.

That night, my stepson and I set up the recorder in hopes of getting some EVPs.

I began asking questions like, who are you, why are you hear and do you know you're dead? Then

I proceeded to direct any spirits in the apartment to go to the light.

When we rewound the tape to listen, we heard grunting and even a man saying in a Freddy Krueger style voice, "Get away from the light." But the big breakthrough did not come until the following night. I set up the recorder in the living room with just a dim light. To my left was my very dark kitchen.

In pursuit of more proof, I decided to try aggravating the spirits like was done in the White Noise movie.

Guess what? It worked! I said, "Ohhh this cigarette is good," I told the unseen spirit. "Want some? Oh, that's right; you're dead. You can't have any."

At that same moment, I saw off to my left on the kitchen wall, a circle of light appear, with a dark letter 'A' in the middle of it. Then every hair on my body stuck straight up and that was enough for me!

I called my friends who owned the apartment building.

I told them that I was moving and why I was moving. My friends thought I was crazy, but they let me out of the lease. From then on, it seemed that my new ghostly friends did not want me to leave.

As a matter of fact, some may say they were heated over the idea, so much so that I awoke my last morning there to a nasty burning smell, and sat up quickly only to find my blinds off the window and clear across the other side of the bedroom lying on my electric heater melting.

I promptly got up, packed my belongings, and my stepson and I left. We moved down the road where I never had any more problems. Well with apartments anyways.

And I soon remembered that the name of the girl who had died in the fire began with the letter A.

After I left, one of the building's owners decided to take over that same apartment for a few months. However, he ended up selling the building three months later. When I asked why they sold it after just pouring a ton of money into fixing it up, they would not comment. Frank after taking over that apartment would develop health issues that would eventually kill him. Was it related? Well, his brother Don also had a heart attack and some years later so did I.

I am sure there is no connection at all. But perhaps worst of all, that beautiful woman who had come to my apartment, never returned and never even picked up the phone for me again.

I not only believe the paranormal is real, I lived it and this was not my only time.

I have come to a fond respect and understanding when it comes to the paranormal, no matter if you believe or not.

The paranormal is very real. I have had experiences ever since I was a small child and to this day it has only made me want more.

I had two Out of Body experiences when I was just 9 or 10 years old and those weighed on my mind my entire life because these two out of body experiences was much different than the one I would later experience in 2004, I am now forty-four years old, you see the OBE I experienced before I was able to travel outside the room I was in and time did not exist.

As a child, I remember not being able to leave the room both times and in different rooms. After speaking with the thousands of guest and experts on these topics for almost 9 years now, it has made me question my experiences as a child in 1980-81, however, I will get back to that in a moment.

So push ahead to 2004, I was awakened at 3:20 am to a knock on the window, to my surprise it was my mother standing outside the window. She was beautiful and did not look a day over 30. She was 64 when she passed away.

I looked back and my body was lying on the bed and I really thought I was dead.

My mother had no feet, she was levitating inches above the ground floating she put out her hand through the glass, I laid my hand in hers and off we went.

She took me to the home I grew up in, she showed me my father and my sister and my mother gave me messages for the two of them.

She said tell your father I am OK, I am happy, it is not his time, she said "I am with Uncle Joe and There is a God."

My mother had another message before she left me, She told me don't do anything stupid and that everything would be OK and that personal things in my life would change and she was right.

My business grew, my children were with me and my living situation changed for the better just as she told me.

The night ended and she left me back on the other side of that window in my bedroom and that would be that last time I would ever see her.

Several weeks later I received more confirmation. I was at my sisters for a birthday party when going through my sister's scrapbook I come across a picture of my mother dressed the exact same as on that night and looked like a carbon copy. I smiled and thought to myself, yes mom, I believe you.

Today in 2016 I question my OBE'S as a child because as a child I was contained, unable to travel freely. I now wonder if those early experiences were not OBEs but rather abduction.

I see UFOs often and at times it seems like I am the only one who can see them.

That is another book for another chapter sometime I guess.

I will end this the way I end my radio show each night.
Keep your eyes posted to the sky because you never know what you might see and keep your

ears posted to my show because you never know what you might learn.

Maybe one day I can tell my other very real lessons from the other side.

Michael Vara Host/producer
Late Night in the Midlands Radio
www.latenightinthemidlands.com

Joshua, a Hero Named Jack, and Baby Hope

Karen Anderson

Can an elderly cat bring through a message from a messiah? Is it possible for a deceased dog to warn of an unknown but fatal health risk? Can a murdered child provide clues from beyond the grave about her killer? I'll let you decide after reading my most amazing paranormal encounters.

As an Animal Communicator, Psychic and Medium I get to experience all kinds of strange, unusual and unexplained phenomenon. I communicate with departed human and animal spirits from the Other Side on a daily basis, so my 'normal' day is probably a bit abnormal for most. While each session is unique and different, I've selected my most memorable experiences to share with you.

What I love about my work is that I never know who will show up for a session or what messages will come through. I am humbled and amazed by these experiences and so grateful to be a part of this journey.

Joshua

In 2007, I had a telephone session with a client named Carol, who lived in Spokane, Washington. Her primary goal was to check in with her 16-year-old kitty, Minx, to see how she was feeling. The sweet little calico was on medication for arthritis and kidney disease which can be extremely painful. I began the session with Minx and soon messages started to come through. The kitty seemed to be doing well for her age and shared a minimum level of discomfort. I relayed all the information to Carol, who was relieved to hear that the medications were doing their job.

We were just about ready to close down the session when I sensed an immense energy entering from my right-hand side. This enormous light-filled being appeared without any warning, but I immediately felt an overwhelming sense of love emanating from him. There were many different religious references all around him and in his auric field. Among them, I saw a symbolic cross, a church and there was a brilliant white-gold light illuminating around him. I could see his soft facial features including his eyes, his brow, and a comforting smile. I was a bit unnerved as I had never had such an angelic being like this come through before. It was like being on an incredible magic carpet ride as his radiant energy swirled around me like a soft blanket of love. I told Carol that someone was coming through for her and asked if she was open to hearing from whoever this was. Carol anxiously said yes and I focused my energy on this unexpected visitor.

"Joshua, do you know a Joshua?" I asked.

This very impressive light-being was so large his energy filled my entire office. His face was a shimmering white-gold that moved in and out of focus. I could feel his eyes looking down upon me which made me feel completely safe and protected. Whoever this was had some incredible power that radiated the purest love I had ever felt.

I kept hearing that name repeating in my head. Joshua. His was very polite and respectful as he waited for me to focus. Not all spirit people are this patient or kind; in fact, some spirits will rush into a session and get right in my face. He did none of those things.

"I feel a bit embarrassed. I was raised Catholic, and I think this may be one of the disciples, but I'm just not sure. Maybe even a saint. Do you know of a very saintly being named Joshua?"

"I think so," came Carol's reply. "Is there a message?"

"Yes, he says that he answered your prayers and your sister is going to be just fine. Does that make any sense to you?" I sent love to Joshua and asked him to tell me more, but nothing else came through.

"Actually, it does!" she gasped. "I know exactly who that is. Tell him thank you so much and we are all so grateful for everything he has done. Oh my goodness, I can't believe this!"

I got a huge wave of goosebumps at that moment which usually signifies that spirit energy is nearby or surrounding me.

"Okay, I'll tell him," I said, as I turned my attention back toward Joshua. Within a split second, the energy brightened and then vanished just a quickly as it appeared.

"Wow, Carol, he's gone. Who was that? Who's Joshua?"

"Well, it's not Joshua. It's 'Yeshua'. You see I'm Jewish, and I pray to 'Yeshua.'"

"Sorry, but I don't know who that is," I said. "I've never heard of anyone named 'Yeshua' before. Is he a saint?"

"Well, you could say that!" Carol said with a laugh. "Yeshua is the Jewish name for 'Jesus.'"

Everything went quiet.

"Jesus? As in the one and only Jesus Christ?" I asked slowly realizing who was just here in my office.

"That's the one!" Carol answered. "My sister was diagnosed with cancer about a year ago, and I've been praying to Yeshua every day to send her healing. Those are the prayers that Yeshua said he answered. The cancer is now in remission, and she's doing great!"

The energy of Jesus was just here! Even though I didn't know who he was, he trusted me to deliver his message. Oh, this is going to go over real well when I get to the pearly gates someday.

It's In the Glands

Marilyn and her husband, Brad contacted me when their beloved boy Jack, a 200 lb. English Mastiff, passed away. They were heartbroken when they lost their beautiful and devoted friend and wanted me to check in with him and make sure he was okay on the Other Side.

Jack was very easy to connect with, and his energy came through feeling light, bright and very happy. He was sweet and funny and spoke to me about his deep love for his human family. Jack told me his passage to the Other Side had been effortless. He said to tell his human mom and dad that he had no regrets about it being his time to go. He said his huge body had finally failed him, and he was tremendously grateful that they helped him make his transition.

About six months earlier, Jack developed inoperable cancer and sadly there were no other options for the 13-year-old boy. The only thing left to do was, to say their goodbyes. They made the appointment for euthanasia with their veterinarian and lay on the floor with him right up to his last breath. It's an impossible decision, and none of us ever want to be the one to make that call. But it is part of our contract with our animal loved ones, and they entrust us with their well-being and sometimes they need us to intervene.

During the session, Jack mentioned a very special painting of him that hung over the fireplace. He described it to me in great detail mentioning the main colors and how much he loved it. Marilyn and Brad were speechless as they had commissioned a painting of Jack after he died and had indeed hung it proudly over the fireplace. This message struck a chord with

Marilyn and Brad. The fact that their deceased dog could see the painting and know exactly where it was placed was nothing less than mind boggling. The session was coming to an end when Jack sent me a very strange message.

"Talk about having trouble sleeping," he said. "Okay, this is strange, and I'm not sure what this means," I announced. "Jack wants me to mention that one of you is having trouble sleeping."

"That would be me," came Marilyn's reply. "I've had a hard time sleeping lately. Why do you ask?"

"Well, I'm not sure. Jack just told me to mention it. Let me see if he can tell me anything else."

I turned my attention toward Jack's energy.

"What's up with the sleeping issue, Jack?" I asked him quietly in my mind.

"It's in the glands," came his urgent reply. "Tell her it's in the glands."

I repeated the message to Marilyn and Brad stressing the feeling of urgency and finished up the session. I didn't give it another thought until about two months later when I received an email from Marilyn:

"Karen, I wanted to let you know what has happened since we last spoke. If you recall, Jack told me to check my glands during our phone call. I didn't say anything at the time, but I had been having a lot of health issues in the months leading up to that session. I had been to doctors and specialists trying to figure out what was wrong with me to no avail. Like Jack said, I had trouble sleeping which was true among other things, but no one could figure out exactly what was wrong. After his message to 'check the glands,' I went back to my oncologist and told them to take another look. The doctor agreed, and the test results confirmed the worst possible news. It turns out I have advanced breast cancer. We are baffled as to why it didn't show up on any prior tests; biopsies or mammograms and the doctors had all but ruled it out. Had it not been for Jack's message I wouldn't have pursued it with my doctors and it would have been too late. I'm scheduled for surgery next week. I'm having a double mastectomy. I just wanted you to know how much I appreciate you and the work you do. If it weren't for you, I just might not have caught this in time. Thank you, Karen. Thank you so very, very much!"

I was truly shocked. When Jack's urgent message, 'it's in the glands', came through, I didn't think much more about it. I delivered the message and closed down the session. Now Marilyn was faced with advanced breast cancer, radiation, and chemotherapy treatments. No one knew if she would make it through this or not but at least now she had a chance.

Over the next few months, Brad kept me posted on Marilyn's surgery and the recovery process. She made it through the long procedure and was now facing the devastating effects of chemotherapy and radiation. Marilyn boldly posted bald photos of herself on her Facebook page, and we all rallied around her and sent daily prayers for her recovery.

It was going to be a long, tough battle but Marilyn was a special kind of lady and if anyone could beat cancer, she could. As you can imagine, it would turn out to be the fight of her life. I am happy to report that as I write this Marilyn is alive and well and has been cancer free for over nine years. One message from her deceased dog, Jack, saved her life. What messages await you?

Baby Hope

The nude, decomposing body of a young female child was found stuffed in an ice chest near the Henry Hudson Parkway in Manhattan, New York in 1991. No one came forward to claim the child. No missing child reports were filed. The body was so badly decomposed it was impossible to identify her.

Frustrated by the lack of any solid witnesses or leads, New York Police Department detectives had no choice but to let the case go cold in 1993. Fellow officers and detectives at the 34th Precinct gathered donations and held a funeral service for the little girl they dubbed, 'Baby Hope' and over 200 people attended. My friend, Angel Nieves, was an NYPD detective at that time, and this case was near and dear to his heart. Who could do this to an innocent child?

In 2007, Angel and I had become fast friends after discovering our common love of animals through a random Facebook post. We immediately clicked and often shared insights on our past law enforcement cases or animals in need. I was a former deputy sheriff from Park County, Colorado nothing made me happier than catching a thief, criminal or murderer and putting them behind bars. Now retired from NYPD, Angel gained worldwide notoriety for his role on the popular show Rescue Ink based in Long Island, New York. He was one of the eight tattooed motorcycle riders who rescued animals in need and worked to combat animal cruelty in the city.

Angel and I made a great team. We shared a passion for solving cold cases, and we often collaborated and pooled our knowledge and experience to help bring closure and peace to victims and their families. We donated many hours working late into the night trying to get that one clue that could lead to a break in the case. I would connect psychically with the deceased victims to obtain bits and pieces of information that could be relevant to the case. Angel used his uncanny gut instincts from a lifetime in law enforcement to get into the minds of the suspects and come up with possible scenarios.

In May of 2010, Angel sent me the police sketch of what they thought Baby Hope might look like and said, 'Hey partner, I've got a case I need your help on.' He gave me the only known facts at that time; the victim was female, possibly underweight, three to five years old, dark wavy hair, possibly Hispanic, found in an ice chest.

I sat down at my desk and took a deep breath. I could feel the anger rising in my throat. I had to push it all back so I could focus on Baby Hope's energy which, surprisingly, came right through. It was extremely heartbreaking to feel her sorrow, fear, and sadness. At that time, it never even occurred to me that she may not even speak English.

I made a list of all the information and messages that Baby Hope gave me and emailed it to Angel on February 17th, 2010:

A male family member killed her. Another female knows about this. This man is very abusive; verbally, physically, sexually He raped her, burned her, I feel extreme pain.

She sees him as a father figure, so maybe stepfather or mom's boyfriend Says she didn't know her real father I get a 'J' name like Jorge, Jose I hear a 'C' or 'K' name like Calderon. This man has a hypnotic stare, dark eyes, Hispanic/South American, small man, no more than 5 ft 7 in, thin build. Poor family, meager existence, I hear metal banging clanging, someone works in a laundry or cleaning capacity.

My mommy calls me her 'little angel' I get an 'A' name for her, Angel, Angelica I smell plastic or trashy smells This feels like a torturous life This man is in the Bronx area not far from crime scene

The messages poured in from Baby Hope's energy, and I felt nauseated after typing it all out. What a despicable piece of worthless human being this man was. I sat back in my office hoping that just one of my clues could help catch this killer.

Two years would go by without a word about Baby Hope. Angel emailed me one day and told me that one of the original detectives on this case, Mark Tebben, had retired and a new detective, Robert Dewhurst, was assigned to the case. The news brought back a wave of sadness to me, and I could feel Baby Hope's desperation lingering around my office. Maybe, just maybe, there will be a break in the case. What we needed was for someone to come forward.

Finally in 2013, I received a long-awaited email from Angel. He wrote, "There's been an arrest in the Baby Hope case." He sent me a link to the story with Detective Jerry Giorgio sharing the long-awaited news. The headline read, 'Cousin Arrested In Baby Hope Killing After 22 Years...'

Hallelujah! I got goosebumps all over my body and a feeling of exhilaration pumped through my veins. 'Yes!' I yelled as I poured through the article.

Angel called and said, "You were right on, partner!" his voice was filled with excitement.

"Baby Hope's name is Anjelica. You got her name exactly right and bunch of other stuff too! You said her name was Angel or Angelica, and there was a 'C' name. Her last name is Castillo.

Have you seen the article?" his booming voice was like music to my ears.

"No way! I'm reading it right now," I said. I studied the news release and was shocked to see how many details of case matched my notes from Baby Hope:

Baby Hope's real name was Anjelica Castillo. She was about four years old and Hispanic origin. The murderer, who confessed to killing her, was her cousin, Conrado Juarez. There was a sister who helped him dispose of the body Juarez, originally from Mexico, had tortured and raped Anjelica and starved her before suffocating her. Anjelica's real father had abandoned her Juarez was a small man, dark eyes and stood barely 5 foot 2 inches tall. He worked as a dishwasher on a meager existence and lived in Astoria near the area where the body was found. After he had murdered her, he put Anjelica's body in a trash bag

With this exciting news, I immediately felt Anjelica's energy come through. I could see her dancing around in a pretty little white dress with black shoes. Her long dark hair was pulled back neatly into a ponytail. There was no more sorrow, no more sadness, there was only love coming through. Anjelica turned toward me, smiled and skipped away holding a white daisy in her hand.

Animal Communicator - Psychic – Medium and Author of "Hear All Creatures!"
www.KarenAnderson.net

If you enjoyed our stories please leave us a review on Amazon.

30913517R00089

Made in the USA
San Bernardino, CA
26 February 2016